BY THE SAME AUTHOR
Published by The Young Churchman Co.

"A JOURNEY GODWARD." An Autobiography. Cloth, $2.50.
"PUSEY AND THE CHURCH REVIVAL." Cloth, 50 cts.
"FOND DU LAC TRACTS," five numbers. Sample set, 60 cts.
"THE ROMAN QUESTION." Comprising four pamphlets bound together in one volume, cloth, $1.00.

Published by Longmans, Green & Co.

"CHRISTIAN AND CATHOLIC." Cloth, $1.50.
"A CATHOLIC ATLAS." Royal 8vo, cloth, $2.50.

THE LINEAGE

THE SANCTUARY, ST. PAUL'S CATHEDRAL, LONDON.

THE LINEAGE

From Apostolic Times

of the

American Catholic Church

Commonly Called

the

EPISCOPAL CHURCH

By

THE RIGHT REV. C. C. GRAFTON, S.T.D.
Bishop of Fond du Lac

MILWAUKEE
THE YOUNG CHURCHMAN COMPANY

COPYRIGHT BY
THE YOUNG CHURCHMAN CO.,
1911.

TO

RT. REV. DANIEL SYLVESTER TUTTLE, D.D.,
PRESIDING BISHOP OF THE CHURCH,
GREAT MISSIONARY, WISE ADMINISTRATOR, FAITHFUL RULER,
AND LOVING FRIEND,
WITH THE SINCERE REGARDS OF HIS SERVANT
AND BROTHER IN CHRIST,

CHARLES CHAPMAN GRAFTON, S.T.D., LL.D.,
BISHOP OF FOND DU LAC.

CONTENTS.

THE PREFACE	ix
CHRONOLOGICAL TABLE	xiii

CHAPTER.

I.—THE CHURCH AND ITS FOUNDATION		1
II.—THE APOSTOLIC CHURCH		22
III.—THE CHURCH IN BRITAIN		45
IV.—FORMATION OF THE CHURCH OF ENGLAND		78
V.—THE DIVISION, EAST AND WEST		120
VI.—THE RISE AND DEVELOPMENT OF THE PAPACY		148
VII.—THE CHURCH OF ENGLAND IN THE MIDDLE AGES		190
VIII.—THE REFORMATION IN ENGLAND		215
IX.—DECADENCE AND REVIVAL		250

ILLUSTRATIONS.

The Sanctuary, St. Paul's Cathedral, London—FRONTISPIECE	
Martyrdom of St. Alban	52-53
St. Columba at Oronsay	58-59
Iona at the Present Day	66-67
St. Aidan Preaching to the Northumbrians	80-81
Gregory and the English Slaves	98-99
St. Augustine and the British Bishops	100-101
Murder of Monks by the Danes, Crowland Abbey	108-109
St. Dunstan Reproving King Edwy	110-111
Troitza Monastery, Kremlin	120-121
St. Saviour's Church, Moscow	128-129
The Kazan, St. Petersburg	132-133
An Iconastasis	134-135
Norman Thanksgiving for Victory after the Battle of Hastings	190-191
Murder of St. Thomas à Becket	194-195
Archbishop Langton Producing before the Barons the Charter of Henry I.	200-201
The Seven Bishops Sent to the Tower	246-247
A Modern Altar and Reredos	250-251

PREFACE.

DEAR READER:

Let me fall back on the good old-fashioned form of Preface, and ask your indulgent perusal of this book and your interest in it. You will find some points with which you disagree. It would be impossible that it should not be so. Do not, however, for some few facial blemishes, condemn the work as worthless. Give credit to the motive of the writer, and help on the good work it is hoped by it to do.

The book is a gift to the Church in aid of the laity. It was undertaken because there is a large body of laymen who have but an imperfect grasp on the history of the Church. They have not time to read any of the larger works, and the facts they know are not held in true perspective. Here they have in small compass an outline of the history of their Church: a brief sketch of the foundation of the Apostolic period, the Church in Britain, the Celtic period, the division of East and West, the development of the Papacy, the Church in the Middle Ages, the Reformation, the decadence of the Church, and her revival.

My brother clergy often complain of the lack of zeal on the part of their laymen. But how can we expect them to take an interest in the Church of which they know so little? Must we not teach our children of the costly struggle that obtained our independence or preserved our nationality? To inspire loyalty, must we not fly the flag over the schoolhouse, and encourage the singing of patriotic songs? If our laity are not to rest content with a mere outward conformity to the Church, but are to love it, they must know of its past struggles, and the present one in which it is engaged. We must seek to arouse in them an enthusiasm for the Church, such as burned in the hearts of the confessors and martyrs, doctors and ancient Bishops. Christ came to send a fire on earth. It should burn within our hearts. In contrast with any other cause, it should be the great Cause of our lives.

If, my dear clerical brother, you wish to build up an active parish, you will find it profitable to distribute this book among your people. The author makes nothing financially by it. He has produced it for the benefit of the Church, and of his brother clergy. Surely some guild or friend can be found who will furnish the small means required for its distribution.

We send it out, invoking God's blessing on it and on its readers. Whatever there is of good in the work, may God bless to the Church's profit, and overrule whatever there may be of error. It has been written, we would humbly say, in loyalty to our Church, and in dependence upon the Holy Spirit.

A CHRONOLOGICAL TABLE.

A. D.
- 33. Day of Pentecost.
- 43. Invasion of Britain by Julius Caesar.
- 54. Family of Caractacus hostages at Rome.
- 55. St. Paul prisoner at Rome.
  St. Paul's possible visit to Britain.
- 170. Missionaries from Gaul.
- 304. Martyrdom of St. Alban.
- 314. Council of Arles, British Bishops present.
- 325. General Council of Nicea.
- 347. British Bishops at Council of Sardica.
- 381. General Council of Constantinople.
- 400. St. Ninian, Missionary to Scotland.
- 410. Evacuation of Britain begun by Romans.
- 427. Pelagian Controversy; aid sought from Gaul.
- 428. Invasion by the Picts, and Alleluia Battle.
- 431. General Council of Ephesus.
- 447. Visit of Gallican Bishops. Pelagianism defeated.
- 450-550. Destruction of churches by Northern Barbarians.
- 451. General Council of Chalcedon.
- 477. Invasion by Angles, Jutes, and Saxons begun.
- 547. Settlement of Angles in Northumbria.
- 553. General Council of Constantinople.
- 565. Columba settles in Iona.
- 587. The Heptarchy established.
- 590. Pope Gregory begins extension of the Roman Patriarchate.
- 597. Augustine lands in Kent.

603. Conference between Augustine and British Bishops.
604. Augustine died. The succession from him eventually died out.
616. East Saxons reject the Faith; recover it in 654.
669. Archbishop Theodore lands in Britain, and unites the Churches.
673. Synod of Hertford. Ten ancient Rules of Discipline accepted.
678. Wilfrid appeals to Rome against Theodore's division of his Diocese.
680. Synod of Hatfield; Decrees of the Five General Councils received.
681. Parochial system founded.
716. Boniface of Exeter becomes a missionary in Friesland.
787. Synod of Chelsea; the Catholic Faith declared.
787. First Danish invasion in the North.
795. Danes destroy Lindisfarne Monastery.
835. Egbert defeats the Danes at Hengist's Down.
866. Danes make a planned invasion and destroy the Anglo-Saxon Churches.
878. Danes defeated; leave or become Christians.
879. Alfred codifies the laws of his kingdom.
890. Co-equal intercourse of English and foreign churches.
1017-1035. King Cnut and his Son.
1042-1066. Edward the Confessor.
1055. Great Schism between East and West of Christendom.
1066. Struggle between Harold and William the Norman.
1066-1087. William I., the Conqueror.
1067. William I. forbids receipt of papal letters without leave.
1070. William the Conqueror refuses homage to the papacy.
1073-1085. Pope Gregory VII. (Hildebrand).
1085. Osmund, Bishop of Sarum, compiles his liturgy.

1087-1100. William II.
1095. Peter the Hermit preaches the first crusade.
1100-1135. Henry I.
1107. Henry I. agrees to compromise the question of investiture.
1115. Welsh Bishops become united to Canterbury.
1119. The Pope invades the rights of the See of Canterbury.
1135-1154. Stephen or Maud.
1154-1189. Henry II.
1164. Constitutions of Clarendon.
1170. Conflict of Church and State ends. Murder of Becket.
1189-1199. Richard I.
1198-1216. Innocent III. becomes Pope from 1198 to 1216. The culmination of papal claims.
1199-1216. John.
1212. Innocent III. deposes King John.
1215. Barons and Stephen Langton, Archbishop of Canterbury, formulate Magna Charta.
1216-1272. Henry III.
1226. Pope Honorius III. demands patronage of English benefices.
1229. Gregory IX. demands a tenth of English property.
1247. Grossetete resists the papal demands.
1256. Pope claims "annates" or first fruits from English Clergy.
1272-1307. Edward I.
1307. The parliament at Carlisle protests against papal exactions.
1307-1327. Edward II.
1309-1378. The Popes reside at Avignon in France.
1317. Pope John XXII. claims eighteen English Bishoprics.
1327-1377. Edward III.

THE LINEAGE OF

1343. The Pope "provides" two Cardinals for England.
1344. The English Commons petition against the Pope's action.
1351. First statute of Provisors against papal patronage.
1353. First statute of Præmunire against papal jurisdiction.
1366. Wycliffe defends refusal of subsidy to Rome.
1377. Wycliffe summoned to trial at St. Paul's for "heresy."
1377-1399. Richard II.
1378-1417. The great schism and decadence of papal power.
1390. Statutes of Provisors re-enacted.
1393. Statutes of Præmunire re-enacted.
1399-1413. Henry IV.
1413-1422. Henry V.
1414-1418. Council of Constance deposes Popes John XXII. and Benedict XIII.
1417-1418. Pope Martin V. nominates thirteen foreign Bishops to England.
1422-1461. Henry VI.
1453. Constantinople taken by the Turks.
1461-1483. Edward IV.
1473. Caxton begins to print at Westminster.
1483-1485. Richard III.
1485-1509. Henry VII.
1509-1547. Henry VIII.
1510. Marriage of Henry VIII. with his brother's widow by papal dispensation.
1512. Dean Colet advocates Church reform.
1516. Erasmus publishes Greek Testament.
1527. Negotiations commenced for Henry's divorce.
1532. Appeals to Rome forbidden.
1534. Convocation declares against papal jurisdiction as of divine right.
1534. Payment of first fruits to Rome forbidden.
1534. Convocation pleads for translation of Bible.

THE AMERICAN CATHOLIC CHURCH. xix

1536. Ten Articles published of Catholic character.
1543. "Necessary Doctrine and Erudition for any Christian Man," put forth by Convocation.
1553-1558. Mary Tudor, Queen.
1556. Cranmer and Ridley burnt for heresy, and succeeded by Pole.
1558-1603. Elizabeth, Queen.
1559. Consecration of Parker and other Bishops.
1560. Pope offers to sanction English Liturgy if supremacy acknowledged.
1563. (Nov. 11th) Last meeting of Council of Trent.
1568. First dissenting Community (Brownists) founded.
1570. Pius V. excommunicates Elizabeth—Roman secession.
1572. First Presbyterian congregation in England (Cartwright's).
1572. Massacre of St. Bartholomew.
1580. Jesuits come to "convert" England and start a schism.
1587. Sixtus V. sanctions hostilities against Elizabeth.
1588. (July) Destruction of Spanish Armada.
1592. Presbyterianism established in Scotland.
1603-1625. James I.
1604. Hampton Court Conference; Canons ecclesiastical published.
1608. First permanent settlement in America.
1611. The Authorized Version of the Bible published.
1625-1649. Charles I.
1642. Civil war begins.
1645. Execution of Archbishop Laud (Jan. 10).
1645. Directory substituted for proscribed Liturgy.
1645. Charles I. declines to "establish" Presbyterianism.
1646. Charles I. refuses to sanction abolition of Episcopacy.
1649. Execution of Charles I. (Jan. 30).
1649-1685. Charles II.

1649. *The Commonwealth* proclaimed (May 19).
1655. Cromwell's persecuting edict issued.
1660. Convention invites Charles II. to return.
1660. Restoration of Charles II. and the Church.
1661. The Savoy Conference between the Bishops and Presbyterians.
1679. Scotch puritans murder Archbishop Sharp.
1685-1688. James II.
1686. Chapels royal opened for Romanist worship.
1686. Massey, a Romanist, made dean of Christchurch, Oxford.
1687. Fellows of Magdalen College replaced by Romanists.
1688. Trial and acquittal of the seven Bishops (June 30).
1689. Declaration of Right (Jan. 22).
1689-1702. William III. (and Mary).
1689. Attempt to remodel the Liturgy by Parliament averted.
1698. Society for Promoting Christian Knowledge founded.
1701. Society for Propagating the Gospel founded.
1702-1714. Queen Anne.
1702. Scotch Parliament re-establishes Presbyterianism.
1703-1791. John Wesley, founder of Methodism.
1714-1727. George I. ⎫
1727-1760. George II. ⎬ The Church in its decadence.
1760-1830.—George III. ⎭
1760. Methodists begin to administer Sacraments.
1784. Consecration of Bishop Seabury for America.
1820-1830. George IV.
1827. The Christian Year, by Keble, published.
1830-1837. William IV.
1833. Tractarian movement began.
1834. Keble's Assize Sermon beginning of Tractarian Movement.
1834. Rejection of bill to relieve Bishops from legislation.
1837. Accession of Queen Victoria.

1843. Secession from the Established Church in Scotland. and founding of Free Kirk of Scotland (Presbyterian).
1849. The Gorham case, involving doctrines on Baptism.
1850. The Roman Church established in diocesan form by Papal Bull.
1856. Decree by Pope of Immaculate Conception of Blessed Virgin.
1864. First diocesan conference, held at Ely.
1864. Convocation condemns "Essays and Reviews."
1866. Convocation condemns Dr. Colenso's writings.
1867. First Pan-Anglican synod, 76 Bishops present.
1869. *Irish Church Disestablishment Act* Passed.
1869. Vatican Council promulgates new doctrine, Papal infallibility.
1870. Vatican Council declares Pope *infallible.*
1908. Fifth Pan-Anglican Conference.

CHAPTER I.

THE CHURCH AND ITS FOUNDATION.

LET US begin the Lineage of our American Church with a little theology.

The Church is the end of God's original design in creating. God designed the Universe that now is, as a preliminary to creating the Church. He created the material Universe and man, that He might eventually develop out of the existing order of things, a new organism. The Church is this new organism. It is the primary purpose and the ultimate object of the creative activity.

Let us next make clear what we mean by the "Church." It is a *spiritual organism*. Philosophers have believed in a future state of reward and punishment, who have had no conception of the Church as the finally developed end of Creation. Many Christians, in like manner, believe in a heaven as a place of reward for good people.

They think of it as a place where they may wander about and do much as they will. They have little idea of its awful sanctity, its law of life, its organization as completing the creative purpose. Heaven is not merely a place, but it is also a new state of life. It is a new mode of union with God. It is thus, the final development of Creation. Its members form together a spiritual organism.

Again: the Church is not a mere *human institution*. Some have thought of it as such. To them it belongs to the same class as other human societies. It is like a kind of fraternal society, similar to that of the Masons, Oddfellows, or Knights of Pythias. It is thus a temporary and earthly society, like a political one, or a society having some philanthropic aim. It is simply a man-made association for some religious purposes. It is only to last as long as the world lasts. It is human in its origin, and only for a time. Is not this the popular Protestant idea?

Again: the Church is not merely *a divine Society*. Some, because it was founded on earth by a Divine Founder, conceive of it as such. They moreover, liken it unto an earthly Kingdom, and claim for it a visible, earthly head. This is the

Roman idea, and tends to concentrate and confine the view of it to this earth. But the Church of Christ is something more than a divinely founded society. It has a wider than an earthly vision. It consists of all the saints in glory, the vast body in the Expectant state, and the few who form the Church Militant on earth. All three together make a spiritual organism which is the Church, of which Christ is the Head.

We must thus realize the fact that, out of our temporary probationary state, God is calling and perfecting souls, who, united to Christ, form a great, grand, spiritual organism. It is not a mere organization. Organizations man can make. God only can make an organism. An organism is something that has life in itself, and can communicate life. . . "At Pentecost, God breathed into the Church the Spirit of Life. It became changed from a lifeless into a living body."[1] Of this spiritual organism which is the Church, the God-Man, Jesus Christ, is the Head, and the Holy Ghost is the Heart. You may conceive of it as a great sphere of light, of which Christ is the Sun, and as filled with the Holy Ghost as its atmosphere. Or

---

[1] *Title Deeds Church of Eng.*, Garnier.

you may think of it as a Temple in which Christ dwells, and of which, united to Him, we are living stones. It is a great and pregnant truth that, what God is to the material universe, namely, the energy immanent within it, Christ, the God-Man, is to the new creation. The Church is thus a living organism, which has life in itself, and can communicate life.

In its final and completed state, when Christ shall come again, the Church will rise into its perfected condition, when all evil and sorrow will for ever cease. Sorrow and sin will be no more.

All the saints, having attained to the Beatific Vision, will then be kept from sinning by that new union with God in Christ, and in blessedness consequently will ever reign. God came into this world, not to make it the good world, but, out of this world, to make a world that would be good.

This spiritual organism, where the creature endowed with free will will then be upheld in God, is the final end of creation. It is being evolved out of the present preparatory state, and is the Church. It is the One, Holy, Catholic, Apostolic Church, which we profess in the Creeds. It is called in Holy Scripture the "Bride of Christ."

together in one all things, in Christ, both which are in heaven and which are on earth."[2] Christ did not come to destroy the Old Dispensation, but He came to fulfil and build upon it. The old was like the six waterpots filled with water, which were to be changed into the wine of the Gospel. God ever thus develops the new order out of the preceding one. Some think that we have little or nothing to do with the Old Testament. But it declares His Mind who changes not. Its moral principles remain the same. The Old Testament reveals, also, the principles of worship. It shows how God would be approached by His Church. The Jewish Dispensation is thus like the bud, of which the Gospel is the unfolded flower.

Among other likenesses, the Old and New Dispensations had each a special Priesthood. The whole of Israel was, we read, a nation of prophets, kings, and priests unto the Lord. The Christian Church was formed in like manner. It was to be a holy nation, a royal priesthood.[3] The distinction between the laity and the clergy, it may be remarked, is not one of kind but of degree. All

---
[2] Eph. i. 10.
[3] I. St. Peter ii. 5, 9.

Christians, baptized and confirmed, partake of Christ's three offices, and exercise prophetical, priestly, and royal powers. But, just as there was in Israel a special order of priesthood, so it is in the Christian Church. The universal gift does not preclude the existence of a specially designated one. And so in each dispensation, there is a special order of priesthood, to invade whose rights and powers is to bring upon the invaders for so doing, the condemnation of Korah, Dathan and Abiram.[4] "When it is understood," said Professor Salmon, "that the scriptural conception of the Church is not that of an aggregate of particles, identical in nature like grains of sand, but of an organized body, the parts of which have differentiated functions, there is no difficulty in receiving the doctrine that the Church is a corporate body, having its rules and officers, and that there are some of its members to whom the special function is assigned of teaching and directing others."

The Christian Ministry.

The reason why sectarians object to receiving Episcopal ordination is because they have an in-

---
[4] St. Jude ii.

perfect grasp of the Incarnation. God became Incarnate that, through union with the Incarnate One, here by grace, we should attain in Him hereafter to a union with God in glory. It was therefore necessary there should be both an Agent, viz: the Holy Spirit, and also means adapted to our dual nature, viz: the sacraments, by which this union with Christ should be effected. The necessity of sacraments implied the further necessity of an authorized ministry to administer them. The mode of ordering and transmission of the ministry is witnessed by the custom of the Spirit-endowed Church. The custom throughout the ages, in the Apostolically descended churches, bears witness to the Episcopal manner of ordination. The character of the ministry, as the representative of Christ, is witnessed by the mode of His instituting it.

It is thus interesting to see how Christ trained the Apostles, and formed the ministry which was to be the authorized representative of Himself. His public life, we may observe, was divided into three parts. The first, in which He exercised especially His public prophetical ministry, begins with His Sermon on the Mount and ends with the Glory of the Mount of Transfiguration, which symbolizes His being the light of the world. The special time of the exercise of His priestly functions begins with the entering into Jerusalem and the offering of Himself in the upper chamber, and terminates with His "It is finished"[5] on the Mount of Calvary. During the great forty days of His Resurrection, He is seen in His kingly attitude as Conqueror of Death and Hell, and this period terminates on the Mount of Olivet on the day of His glorious Ascension. Now, in each of these periods, He began to associate the Apostles with Himself and His offices, and to commission them. He gave them, in the days when He was teaching, power to teach,[6] and with authority. They are to "bind and loose"[7] by the utterance of the Word, and to declare the coming Kingdom. In the awful period of His priestly action, He associated the Twelve with Himself, and commissioned them as Apostles "to do" or "to offer" the Eucharistic Sacrifice as a Memorial of Himself.[8] In the days of His Resurrection, in the exercise of His kingly

---
[5] St. John xix. 30.
[6] St. Matt. x. 7.
[7] St. John xx. 23.
[8] St. Luke xxii. 19.

sovereignty, He gave mission and jurisdiction to His Apostles throughout the whole world.[9] It was then that He bade them make persons members of the Church by baptism. It was at this time, also, that, breathing on them, He gave them power in His name to remit or retain sins.[10] It was most fitting that this power should be given at this time, because the pardoning power belongs to sovereignty.

But with all this, they were not yet consecrated. Consecration implies a separation of persons from all others, and the bestowing on them of a gift. Our Lord, having ascended to the right hand of power, baptizes at Pentecost His whole Church with fire, and with the Holy Ghost.[11] The Holy Ghost, having first dwelt in Christ (being given without measure unto Him), came from Christ, and filled the whole Church. He entered into all its members. He came from Christ, not as a transitory gift, but as a permanent one. He entered into this organism Christ was forming, never again to leave it. The Holy Spirit gave thereby to each and to all of its members their respective

---

[9] St. Matt. xxviii. 19.
[10] St. John xx. 22, 23.
[11] Acts ii. 2-7.

and necessary gifts. He quickened all souls, uniting them to Christ, and empowering all in different degrees in union with Christ's offices. He gave the Apostles a gift for the exercise of all those functions which they had previously been commissioned by Him to perform. The Apostles became thereby "able ministers of the New Testament," *i.e., enabled* to do all those things which they had previously been commissioned to do.[12] Their consecration was thus made complete. We thus see how both Christ and the Holy Spirit ever dwell in the Church. Their presence in the Church makes it a living organism. "The Church," as Dr. Moberly says, "is the perpetuity of Christ's Presence. It is the living temple of God Incarnate." The Holy Spirit, also, abides in the Church, uniting its members to Christ and empowering its ministers to perform their respective functions.

This process of commission and consecration to the Ministry is emphatically brought out in the case of St. Matthias. The falling away of Judas had made a vacancy in the Apostolic band, which was to consist of twelve members.[13] The Apostles

---
[12] II. Cor. iii. 6.
[13] Acts i. 16-20.

12   THE LINEAGE OF

not having been themselves consecrated (their consecration was not completed till the day of Pentecost), could not consecrate him. All they could do at that time was to discover by lot whom the Lord had chosen to fill the vacancy. The lot having fallen on Matthias, he was numbered among the Eleven. He was thus called and commissioned by Christ through the action of the Apostles. He was not thereby consecrated, he was only numbered with the Apostles.[14] Then, together with the other Apostles, he was consecrated, as they were, by the gift of the Holy Ghost at Pentecost.

The Three Orders.

We must now consider the subsequent formation of the three orders of the Ministry, as Bishops, Priests, and Deacons.

When we study the New Testament, we see that there were at first two special classes of ministers. There were the "Apostles and Prophets," upon whose foundations we are told the Church was built.[15] The Apostles specially bore witness to the Resurrection and the Presence of Christ in the Church, and the prophets to the indwelling of

---
[14] Acts i. 26.
[15] Eph. ii. 20.

the Holy Ghost. This comes out very beautifully in the calling and consecration of St. Paul. Our Lord, having ascended to the right hand of power, appeared to Saul as he journeyed on the road to Damascus. Christ then called and commissioned Saul, as He had formerly the Apostles during the time of His public ministry. The consecration of the Apostles was completed, as we have seen, at Pentecost, when the Holy Ghost was given them. In like manner the consecration of Saul to the Apostleship was subsequently completed. This took place by special order of the Holy Ghost, personally revealing Himself to the prophets at Antioch.[16] Then it was that the Holy Ghost was given to Saul as it had been given to the other Apostles, and he was thus consecrated. He was not, as he said, "an Apostle of men," as chosen by them, neither commissioned by man, but by Jesus Christ. He was subsequently gathered into the Apostolic fellowship,[17] and was recognized as an Apostle, and his jurisdiction to the Gentiles was assigned him.

The order of the original twelve, in its capacity as a witness of the Resurrection, and the distinc-

---
[16] Acts xiii. 2.
[17] Gal. ii. 9.

tive order of prophets, passed; but our Lord had promised to remain with the Apostolic Ministry "unto the end of the world." [18] He also promised the Holy Ghost to the Church[19] to be its Comforter and Guide. Our Lord also had said, "as the Father sent Me, even so send I you." This implies that an authorized Ministry should be established. Its members might be discriminated by their gifts and different employments, as stated in Ephesians iv. 11: "He gave some, Apostles; and some, prophets; and some, evangelists; and some pastors and teachers," or, by their separate ranks or orders, as Bishops, priests, and deacons. So it came to pass that, forced by the needs of the Church, and under the guidance of the Holy Spirit, the Apostolate gathered into union with itself persons clothed with different degrees of ministerial authority. So we find in the Acts the beginning of the order of deacons, who were ordained by the laying-on of the Apostles' hands.[20] Subsequently a second order,[21] that of "elders," arose, ordained by the laying-on of the hands of Titus and Paul. And lastly, as the

---

[18] St. Matt. xxviii. 20.
[19] Bishop Hall's charge on the *Apostolic Ministry*, p. 18. Liddon's *Sermon* at Consecration of Bishop King.
[20] Acts vi. 6.
[21] Titus i. 5.

need arose of an order so associated with the Apostles as to possess the power of ordination, we find apostolic delegates, like Timothy and Titus, thus empowered.[22] Thus St. Paul writes to Titus: "For this cause left I thee in Crete, that thou shouldest set in order the things that are wanting, and ordain elders in every city." In this way the Christian ministry was established, and in a permanent form. We find no proof in Holy Scripture of a congregational or solely presbyterian form of ordination.[23] And, as in the Jewish Church we find three orders, high priests, priests, and Levites, so in the Christian, as guided by the Holy Spirit and witnessed by Him in the common consent, we find the three orders of Bishops, priests, and deacons.

The Christian Priesthood.

Again, we find that in the Christian dispensation the priesthood was preserved. It is sometimes said that the word "Priest" is not applied to the Christian ministry in the Bible. But this is a mistake. In Isaiah lxvi. 21, we find it prophesied in reference to the coming dispensation, that there

---

[22] II. Tim. i. 6.
[23] Wordsworth, *Christian Ministry;* Sanday, *Priesthood;* Moberly, *Ministerial Priesthood.*

should be "priests." All nations were to come, "And I will take of *them*, for priests and for Levites, saith the Lord." Also our Lord Himself is called the High Priest, and "a Priest after the order of Melchisedec." He was not, therefore, to be confounded with priests of human or Jewish origin. For, as it is written in the Hebrews, "if He were on earth, He should not be a priest" at all,[24] *i.e.*, offering gifts according to the law. But as a High Priest, He would have priests under Him, and to them the Church, guided by the Spirit, applied the Greek term ἱερεύς and the Latin term "sacerdos." The question, however, must not be determined merely by the terms used, but by the *powers* given to the Christian ministry. Now we find that the Christian minister has the same powers given him which characterized the Jewish priesthood, and therefore he is a priest in character and office, like those of old.

Like the priesthood of the Old Dispensation, the Christian priest is to teach, bless, rule, intercede, and offer sacrifice. Was it the duty of the Jewish priest to keep knowledge, and to teach?

---

[24] Heb. viii. 4.

Concerning the Christian ministry our Lord said, "He that heareth you, heareth Me." [25] Did the Jewish priest exercise ecclesiastical rule? To the Christian priest it is said: "Whatsoever ye shall bind on earth shall be bound in heaven, and whatsoever ye shall loose on earth, shall be loosed in heaven." [26] Had the Jewish priest the power of reconciliation and excommunication? To the Christian priesthood was given the ministry of reconciliation, that "whosesoever sins they remit, they are remitted, and whosesoever sins they retain, they are retained." [27] Could the Jewish priest stand with his censer between the living and the dead, and stay the plague? "Is any sick among you? Let him call for the elders of the Church, and let them pray over him, anointing him with oil in the Name of the Lord, and the prayer of faith shall save the sick." [28] Did the priest of the old order bless the people in like manner that the Christian priest blesses in Christ's Name? Was the Jewish priest to offer sacrifice? "We have an Altar." [29] An altar involves sacrifice and priesthood, and

---

[25] St. Luke x. 16.
[26] St. Matt. xvi. 19.
[27] St. John xx. 23.
[28] St. James v. 14.
[29] Heb. xiii. 10.

there the Christian priest offers the Eucharistic memorial to God. The whole Christian Church is a priesthood, and the clergy, as its representatives, are priests. St. Paul, in Romans xv. 16, asserts his priestly office in recognized liturgical words. He speaks (we believe we give a true translation) of "the grace that was given to me of God, that I should be the priest of Jesus Christ unto the Gentiles, ministering the work of a priest in respect of the Gospel of God, that the oblation of the Gentiles might be made acceptable, being sanctified by the Holy Ghost." Our Lord Himself, in bidding the Apostles *"do this,"* or, as the word here in connection with liturgical ones signifies, "offer" this, established the Eucharistic Sacrifice.[30] Christ washing the Apostles' feet was part of the service of priestly ordination, as it was of old.[31] The Lord's Supper was not thus the establishment merely of a communion, but a setting forth and a presentation to the Eternal Father of "Our Lord's death, till He come again."[32]

The Christian ministry was thus made the ex-

---

[30] St. Luke xxii. 19.
[31] Lev. viii. 6.
[32] I. Cor. xi. 26.

tension of our Lord's offices as Prophet, Priest, and King. Our Lord in this way continues what He began to do, and abides with us, going about, "doing good." [33] The old priesthood was thus not destroyed; it was simply changed. Thus we are told, "the Priesthood being *changed,* there was of necessity a change of the law." [34] There was a new law of life given, because there was a new Priesthood. The old was enlarged, elevated, spiritualized.

We gather then from Holy Scripture that the general principle concerning the ministry is that the Church, guided by the Holy Spirit, calls or selects those who are to represent it; and Christ, through ordination and consecration, authorizes and bestows His gifts of the Holy Spirit on those who are to represent Him. The received custom in the Church, undisputed for fifteen hundred years, and still held by the larger portion of Christendom, is that the power to ordain lies with the Bishops, as the Apostles' successors. The theory that it might be given by presbyters, or apart from the Apostolically descended ministers, is contrary to the tradition and custom of the Church. And

---
[33] Heb. vii. 12.
[34] Acts x. 38.

it is to be observed, that by ordination not only is a gift and grace betowed; but, by being gathered into the Apostolic fellowship, mission and jurisdiction are also given. In this way, the Christian ministry has come to us Anglicans from Apostolic times. And so it is declared in the preface to the Ordinal in our Book of Common Prayer, that "from the Apostles' times, there have been these orders of Ministry in Christ's Church: Bishops, Priests, and Deacons." Moreover, our Church asserts her belief in the doctrine of the Apostolic succession when she prays, "O Holy Jesus, who hast . . . . promised to be with the ministers of Apostolic succession to the end of the world; Be graciously pleased to bless the ministry and service of him who is now appointed to offer the sacrifice of prayer and praise. . . ." This sacred inheritance entrusted to us by God, is it not our duty to honor, preserve, and guard?

> The twelve Apostles first Christ made
>   His ministers of grace;
> And they their hands on others laid,
>   Ordaining in their place.

> So age by age, and year by year,
>   His grace has never failed,
> For still the Holy Church is here,
>   Though her dear Lord is veiled.

BOOKS CONSULTED AND REFERRED TO IN CHAPTER I.

Wordsworth's and the Speaker's *Commentaries.*
Lange, Sadler, Cornelius A'Lapide, Maldonatus.
Introduction to New Testament. Zahn.
Acts of the Apostles. Ragg.
Acts of the Apostles. Rackham.
Church and the Ministry. Gore.
Christian Tradition. Pullan.
What is Christ's Church? Hammond.
Christian Priesthood. Moberly.
Christian Ministry. Lightfoot.
Remarks on Lightfoot's Christian Ministry. Wordsworth.
Holy Orders. Whitham.
Doctrine of the Priesthood. Carter.
Conception of the Priesthood. Sanday.
Orders and Unity. Gore.
Grace of the Ministry. Denton.

CHAPTER II.

THE APOSTOLIC CHURCH.

THE APOSTLES, having received orders from our Lord to go and teach all nations,[1] baptizing them in the Name of the Father, Son, and Holy Ghost, went everywhere, making disciples. The Church was founded on the day of Pentecost, and began at Jerusalem.[2] It shortly took root at Damascus,[3] and at Antioch,[4] and in Syria. In 53 A.D., we find St. Paul arriving at Ephesus, which was the kernel of Hellenism. We find him next passing over to Macedonia[5] and Greece. He reached Rome, and finally Spain. In his voyage from Rome to Spain, he probably touched the southern portion of Gaul; and Marseilles became the seed plot for extension of the gospel. It thus spread

---
[1] St. Matt. xxviii. 19.
[2] Acts i. 4.
[3] Acts ix. 2.
[4] Acts xi. 20, 21.
[5] Acts xvi. 10, *seq.*

into Spain, and Gaul, and to the farthest bounds of the West. It was probably carried eastward by St. Thomas and other Apostles.[6]

What the teaching of the Apostles was, and what kind of Church government they established, we learn from the New Testament. The Apostles taught that Jesus Christ was the Son of God and the Son of Man.[7] He was the Messiah[8] who came in fulfilment of prophecy. He was born of the Virgin Mary, was crucified, dead and buried,[9] rose on the third day, ascended unto the Right Hand of power,[10] and gave to the Church the Holy Ghost, the Comforter.[11] He was the Lamb of God, the Propitiation, the Mercy Seat, the Sin-Victim, the At-One-Maker, man's only Saviour. He bore our sins in His own body on the tree, and by His stripes we are healed.[12] We are accepted for His sake.

The Apostles did not originate a christology different from that found in the Gospels. During Christ's visible ministry, they had known Him

---
[6] *Ch. of Aposts.*, Ragg, 141-223.
[7] Acts vii. 56.
[8] Acts viii. 37.
[9] Acts ii. 23, 24.
[10] Acts ii. 33.
[11] St. John xvi. 7.
[12] Isa. liii. 5.

"after the flesh."[13] But when the Holy Ghost filled and illuminated them, they saw into the deeper meaning of His life and teaching. They understood the mystery that was hid from ages, and St. Paul and the others, taught by the Holy Ghost, brought it out in their Epistles.

It was not by the works of the law that we could be saved, but by being possessed of the "righteousness of God"[14] made ours in Christ by a living, loving faith. We were to be in Him, and so saved by His merits; and He to be in us, and so the new life principle in us. He was the second Adam,[15] the Head of the new regenerate race. And as in the first "Adam all die, even so," that is by actual communication of nature, "in Christ" were all to be "made alive."[16]

The Apostles preached the doctrine of faith and repentance[17] on man's part, to obtain the benefit of union with Christ; and baptism on Christ's part, as the instrument effecting that union, and bestowing remission of sins. They declared Christ to be the Head of the Church, which was His

---

[13] II. Cor. v. 16.
[14] Rom. i. 16, 17.
[15] I. Cor. xv. 45.
[16] I. Cor. xv. 22.
[17] Acts ii. 38.

mystical Body.[18] And we were not to be saved as individuals apart from the Church, but in it and as members of it. The Church was the Ark into which we were to be gathered. "The Lord added to the Church daily such as should be saved." [19]

We find the Apostles establishing the solemn observance of the Lord's Day,[20] the administration of Baptism,[21] the gift of the Spirit in Confirmation,[22] the reconciliation by Absolution of penitents,[23] and the offering of the Holy Eucharistic Sacrifice.[24] They also took order concerning the Church's worship,[25] its Liturgy,[26] its discipline,[27] and the rule of Holy Living.[28]

The Government of the Church.

As to the government of the Church, the Apostles in all probability received directions from the Lord Himself during the forty days, when "He spoke of the things pertaining to the Kingdom of

---

[18] Eph. iv. 16.
[19] Acts ii. 47.
[20] Acts xx. 7.
[21] Acts ii. 41.
[22] Acts viii. 17.
[23] Acts xix. 18.
[24] Acts xx. 7.
[25] I. Cor. xiv. 23 to end.
[26] Acts ii. 42.
[27] I. Cor. v. 9 to end.
[28] I. Cor. vi. 7 to end.

God." [29] It was but natural that, as the Church grew, its form of government should conform itself to that of the mother Church at Jerusalem. Here we find St. James, the resident local head, surrounded by a band of elders, or presbyters, and deacons. Wherever the Church went, this came to be the established order of local Church government. It was so established in Asia by St. John, who was the accredited organ for the transmission of the mind of the ascended Lord to His Church on earth. It is apparently recognized in the Book of Revelation, where we find each local Church under the supervision of its Angel, or Bishop.[30] It was slower in its development in some places, like Alexandria, where it appears that several had the power of ordination. This might have been adopted as a security that the ordaining power should not fail. Here, as at Corinth, the principles of Episcopal government became, by the guidance of the Holy Spirit, finally established.

Episcopal ordination thus became the rule of the Church, and continued unbroken for 1,500

---
[29] Acts i. 3.
[30] Rev. i. ii. iii.

years. "History," says Bishop Lightfoot, who has sometimes been thought to take an opposite view, "seems to show decisively, that before the end of the second century each Church, or organized Christian community, had its three orders of Bishops, Priests, and Deacons; and it seems vain to deny that in the second century the Episcopal orders were firmly and widely established." [31]

Prof. Harnack wrote: "The Epistles show the monarchical Episcopate so firmly rooted, so highly elevated above all other offices, so completely beyond dispute."

Such was the government of the Church. It was not Congregational, nor Presbyterian, nor Papal, but Episcopal. But while each Church had a certain independency, they together submitted themselves to the government of the general Church. The Apostles, exercising a jurisdictional power, sent St. Paul to the gentiles, and St. Peter to those of the circumcision. The Apostles, as having supreme authority, assembled together in council under the presidency of St. James, with the elders and presbyters at Jeru-

---

[31] Lightfoot, *Christian Ministry*, pp. 12-31.

salem, and decided points of discipline.[32] According to Eusebius,[33] there was a second council after the death of James which elected Symeon as his successor. St. Peter claimed and exercised no supreme authority; but the Church was bound together by divine charity and a common faith, and appealed in need to a general council. And this is the present position of the Anglican Communion.

WITNESSES TO APOSTOLIC TEACHING.

Our space allows the citation of very few authorities. Early among the Fathers was St. Ignatius, who succeeded SS. Peter and Paul at Antioch, and wrote letters to several churches on his way to his martyrdom at Rome. There is no question of the genuineness of his epistles, as has been demonstrated by Bishop Lightfoot. St. Ignatius was a very old man when he wrote about the year 110. He bears witness to the supernatural birth of our Lord, and also to the reality of His human nature, the denial of which was one of the earliest heresies. In his epistle to the Trallians[34] he thus declares that Christ was truly born, and ate and drank,

---
[32] Acts xv.
[33] Euseb., *H. E.*, iii. 11; Lightfoot, *C. M.*, 34.
[34] Ep. ad Trall., Book III., § 9.

that He was truly persecuted under Pontius Pilate, "was truly crucified and died," "and was, moreover, truly raised from the dead." He testifies to the common establishment of the three orders of the Ministry, the acknowledged supremacy of the Bishops, the dutiful subordination required of the Presbyters, the valued services of the Deacons, and the necessity of the maintenance of union with the Apostolic order for the preservation of the Faith.

He writes, "Let all men respect the Deacons of Jesus Christ, even as they would respect the Bishop, as being a type of the Father, and the Presbyters as the Council of God. Apart from these, there is not even the name of a Church."[35] "When," he wrote to the Philadelphians,[36] "I was among you, I spake with a loud voice, with God's own voice, Give ye heed to the Bishop and the Presbytery and Deacons." In his letter to Smyrna, he said, "Do ye all follow your Bishop as Jesus Christ followed the Father, and the Presbytery as the Apostles; and to the Deacons pay respect as to God's commandment. Let no

---
[35] Ep. Tral., III., 3.
[36] Ep. Phil. § 7.

man do aught of things pertaining to the Church apart from the Bishop." "When ye are obedient to the Bishop, as to Jesus Christ, it is evident to me that ye are living, not after man, but after Jesus Christ. . . . It is therefore necessary, even as your wont is, that ye should do nothing without the Bishop; but be obedient also to the Presbytery as to the Apostles."

"As many as are of God and Jesus Christ, they are with the Bishop, and as many as shall repent and enter into the unity of the Church, these also shall be of God, that they may be living after Jesus Christ."

"Be ye careful to observe one Eucharist,[37] for there is one Flesh of our Lord Jesus Christ, and one Cup unto union in His Blood. Obey the Bishop and the Presbytery without distraction of mind, breaking one Bread, which is the medicine of immortality and the antidote that we should not die but live forever in Jesus Christ." "They," speaking of heretics, "abstain from Eucharist, because they allow not that the Eucharist is the Flesh of our Saviour, Jesus Christ, which Flesh

---

[37] Ep. Phil. v. § 4.

suffered for our sins, and which the Father of His goodness raised up."[38]

If we examine the writings of the contemporaries of the Apostles such as St. Barnabas, or those of sub-Apostolic times, men who were trained by the Apostles themselves: SS. Ignatius, Clement, Polycarp, of the first of whom Eusebius records that he was "a disciple of St. John"—we find the same general Apostolic teaching. They bear witness to the Episcopal form of Church government, to the divine origin and grace of the sacraments, and to the liturgical character of the worship of the Church.[39] The connection between the Apostles and these, their followers, is beautifully brought out by St. Papias, a disciple of St. John. "If at any time," he says, "I met with any one who had been a follower of the elders anywhere, I made it a point to enquire what were the declarations of the elders, what was said by Andrew, Peter, or Philip; what by Thomas, James, John, Matthew, or any others of the disciples of our Lord; for I do not think I derived so much benefit from books

---

[38] Ep. Smyrna, § 6.
[39] *Apostolic Fathers*, Wake; *Patristic Study*, Swete; *Age of the Fathers*, Bright.

as from the living voice of those that are still surviving." [40]

Further, we may say concerning the Episcopate, it was held (we quote from Bishop Gore) that "when Hegesipus, the father of Church History, visited the West about A. D. 167, he found a succession of Bishops in each city, and made a list of the Bishops for the purpose of his history at Rome." [41] This fact is cited in Eusebius. [42]

When Irenæus, the great representative of tradition, writes against the Gnostics, about A. D. 180, he regards "Episcopacy as amongst the first principles of the Church, and as the supreme safeguard of the Orthodox faith." [43] Tertullian, about A. D. 200, uses like language and confronts the Gnostic churches with the requirements of the Succession.

So the fathers bear witness to other doctrines. St. Polycarp, Bishop of Smyrna, born A. D. 69 or 70, who lived to be one hundred years old, declares his belief in the Blessed Trinity, which is thus stated in his prayer, shortly before his mar-

---

[40] *Ecc. His.*, Eusebius, Ch. xxxix. p. 125.
[41] *Orders and Unity*, Gore, p. 126.
[42] Euseb., *H. E.*, iv. 22.
[43] *Orders and Unity*, Gore, p. 127.

tyrdom: "True and faithful God, I praise Thee for all Thy mercies; I bless Thee, I glorify Thee, through the Eternal High Priest, Thy beloved Son, Jesus Christ, with Whom, to Thyself and the Holy Ghost, be glory now and for ever and ever. Amen." St. Clement, whose name St. Paul tells us, "is in the book of Life,"⁴⁴ wrote, "Brethren, we ought so to think of Jesus Christ as of God, and as the Judge of the living and the dead."

St. Justin the Martyr, born 103, the noted Christian philosopher, wrote a great apology for Christianity. He bears witness to the liturgical and sacrificial character of Christian worship. He speaks in his Dialogue with the Jew Trypho of those "who, through His name, offer those sacrifices which Jesus Christ commanded to be offered, that is, which are offered by Christians in every part of the world, in the sacrament of bread and wine." He states in his *Apol.* I., "that the bread consecrated for thanksgiving, by the prayer of the Word which is from Him, is, we are taught, the Body and Blood of the Incarnate Jesus." He teaches also that baptism is the instrument of regeneration. "We lead them," *i.e.*, the converts,

---
⁴⁴ Phil. iv. 3.

"to a place where there is water, and there they are regenerated, as we also were, for they are then washed in that water in the name of God the Father, the Lord of the Universe, and of our Saviour Jesus Christ, and of the Holy Spirit. This is done in order that we may obtain in the water remission of the sins which we have before committed, and this washing is called "illumination." Christ was made the author of a new race who are regenerated through Him by water and faith.

But while in all this we have the objective side of Christianity set before us, and the means Christ has ordained for communicating grace, the Fathers ever insisted upon the necessity of a true conversion and a living Faith. External observances, if rested upon, would only be a repetition of the law. Christianity is the dispensation of the Holy Spirit. St. Irenæus, a companion of St. Polycarp, speaks of original guilt as affecting all mankind, and born with them; and says that it is only in and through Christ that it is forgiven. He speaks of baptism as the means by which forgiveness is conveyed, and calls it regeneration. We have here the doctrines of the early Church. Beside them, the theology of modern Protestantism, with its denial of the Episcopacy, Priesthood, and the sacrificial offering of the Eucharist, and sacramental grace, seems a very imperfect representation of the Gospel.

Thus much concerning the doctrinal teaching of the early Church. We shall next consider what was the worship of the Church in those primitive times to which we look for our model.

The Worship of the Church.

It is not only interesting but useful to learn what we may from our scanty records of the time concerning the worship and general service of the early Church. The Apostles, as Jews, were accustomed to two forms of service—that of the Synagogue and that of the Temple. They differed in kind, the Synagogue service being that of reading from the Scriptures, prayer, exhortation, and praise; and the Temple worship being that of sacrifice. These were the two forms which God from the earliest times had ordained, and which the Apostles, under the guidance of the Holy Spirit, were to continue. We find them thus assembling in Solomon's Porch[45] at the hour of prayer, for their common and united devotional

---
[45] Acts iii. 1, 11.

exercises. They assembled daily, probably in the Upper Chamber, for the Holy Eucharist, or Breaking of the Bread.[46] These two forms of service have been continued in the Christian Church, under the two forms of the recitation of the Divine Office, and the offering of the Eucharistic sacrifice of the altar.

As the Holy Communion, when established by our Lord, was preceded by the Paschal Supper, it came about that the Apostles at first connected a social meal, called the Agape or Love Feast, with the Holy Eucharist. But the disorder which arose at Corinth led to St. Paul's stern rebuke, and his taking "order" as he said,[47] concerning the celebration of the Holy Communion. He did this probably in consultation with the other Apostles. Therefore we find these two services presently separated, and at the end of the first century, according to a well-known letter of Pliny to the Roman Emperor, the Christians assembled early in the morning for the celebration of the Eucharist.

Though for a time the Sabbath was kept along with the Lord's Day, eventually the first day of

---
[46] Acts ii. 42.
[47] I. Cor. xi. 34.

the week became the day observed by Christians in obedience to the command to keep one day in seven.[48] As God, through Moses, ordained a day to be kept in commemoration of His work in creation; through the Holy Spirit the Church was guided to keep the first day of the week in commemoration of the beginning of the new Creation. It began by Christ's rising from the dead. To go back to Saturday, as the Seventh-day Adventists have done, is to introduce a decadent Jewish order into the Christian religion.[49]

The order of the Eucharistic service is, according to St. Augustine, set forth in I. Tim. ii. 1,[50] (1) "supplications," before the canon; (2) "prayers," especially at the consecration; followed by (3) "intercessions," between the prayers and the blessing; and lastly, (4) the "thanksgiving," such as our *Gloria in Excelsis* at the end. The authority for using forms of prayer had been given by our Lord, when He said, "After this *manner* pray ye."[51] And that manner was a prescribed form.

Forms of prayer and blessing had been set

---
[48] Acts xx. 7.
[49] Liddon's *Sermon on the Lord's Day*.
[50] I. Tim. ii. 1.
[51] St. Matt. vi. 9.

forth in the old Dispensation also; and early it may have been, that the inspired evangelical hymns of the *Magnificat*,[52] *Benedictus*,[53] and *Nunc Dimittis*,[54] began to be used. As Christ, taking part in the Synagogue service[55] prayed for the departed, the Church followed His example. St. Paul remembers Onesiphorus, who had probably passed away, and prays "that God may have mercy on him in that day." [56] The petition in the Lord's Prayer, "Thy Kingdom come," includes the departed as well as the living here on earth. We know certainly that hymns formed part of the service, for St. Paul speaks of "psalms and hymns and spiritual songs," [57] and that the people took a responsive part by joining in the Amen at the Eucharistic prayer. It is much disputed what kind of bread was used; but it was probably unleavened, as at the time of the Passover all leaven had been put away.[58] It was natural that the mixed chalice should be used; since it was the custom to mix a little water with the cup at the Feast of the Pass-

---

[52] St. Luke i. 46.
[53] St. Luke i. 68.
[54] St. Luke ii. 29.
[55] St. Luke iv. 16.
[56] II. Tim. i. 18.
[57] Eph. v. 19.
[58] Exod. xii. 15.

over. Holy Communion was given in both kinds (I. Cor. x. 16), as commanded; and the Sacrament was reserved and carried to the absent, unable by illness to attend. Clement of Alexandria makes mention, writing at the end of the second century (A. D. 190), of the blessing of the oil for the anointing of the sick as St. James had ordered.[59]

It is not unlikely that lights as a religious symbol were used, for we find it recorded at the Eucharistic celebration at Troas that "there were many lights."[60] Unless there was some religious or symbolical meaning in this, it is not reasonable to suppose that it would find place in an inspired writing.

Lange says: "The word lights includes torches, candles, lanterns, all of which were due to the solemnity of the occasion at Troas. There is nothing to show that the young man who fell down dead was overcome by the lights. The lights, besides being symbolical of Christ as the Light of the World, also connected the celebration with the Last Supper, where lights were a necessity." "The symbolical use of lights prevailed in the Church

---
[59] St. James v. 14.
[60] Acts xx. 8.

from very early times."[61] They were used at the Gospel, St. Jerome says, "as the expression and symbol of joy." Silvia, the traveller, tells of the "huge glass candlesticks, the numerous torches, and the infinite luminaries used in the churches and services on her visit to Jerusalem."[62] It is probable that the vestment which St. Paul left behind at Troas[63] after the celebration, was one used by him in the service. The word used might signify either a vestment of peculiar character or the overgarment which the Apostles would personally wear. It is not, however, likely that St. Paul would leave his outer garment behind when he was about to take a sea voyage, but very naturally, he might have left his Eucharistic vestment, together with the books or parchments needed, in the safekeeping of Carpus, who was probably the ruler in the Synagogue, to be brought to him by Timothy. The two vestments, alb and chasuble, used by many of our clergy, have probably been derived, not from Jewish or Roman sources, but from the ordinary dress of the Apostles. As such, they bear

---

[61] Rackman.
[62] Duchesne, *Origines*, 473.
[63] II. Tim. iv. 13.

witness to their Apostolic origin and the continuity of our Church, and should not be a matter of dissension. St. John, Eusebius relates, wore "a sacerdotal plate," [64] certainly some sacredotal ornament, doubtless a reference, says Lightfoot, "to the metal plate on the High Priest's mitre." "Possibly this," he observes, "was a mitre." And we find Polycrates saying that St. John was a priest, "wearing the mitre." We find that the sign of the Cross came into use quite early, for Tertullian tells us that "in all the ordinary actions of daily life, we trace upon the forehead the sign of the cross." [65]

The ceremony of the kiss of peace[66] was a scriptural injunction. We find that in the church, the men and the women were divided; the women, sitting on one side by themselves, gave and received a kiss of peace amongst themselves, and the men on the other side would do the same thing amongst themselves. It is thus observed that the Church's service was like that of the Old Dispensation, and from the beginning was liturgical, ceremonial, and in a degree choral. The Church was

---
[64] Euseb., Book III., Ch. 31.
[65] Vol. I., p. 166.
[66] Rom. xvi. 16.

of course hampered during the first three centuries by intermittent persecutions. She had, at times, to hide herself in the Catacombs. But she had church buildings and Bishops' residences, and was a visible body. We find, for instance, Paul of Samosata, when deposed in 260, refusing to vacate his church or house.

The Church had received moreover from her ascended Lord, through St. John, the details of the heavenly worship,[67] where God is worshipped in spirit and in truth. So, just as in the Old Dispensation, God had taken Moses up into heaven, and Moses established the Jewish worship after the pattern of things he had seen in the Mount,[68] so God, in the New Dispensation, took St. John up into heaven, and the glorious worship he there beheld became the directory of the Apostolic Church. There St. John found "vestments,"[69] lights,[70] incense,[71] and choral service;[72] and the Church, when she gained her full freedom, developed her worship and ceremonial after the heavenly pattern. Dr. Bright has forcibly brought home the lesson in his noble poem on Ritual:

---

[67] Rev. iv.
[68] Ex. xxv. 34.
[69] Rev. iv. 4.
[70] Rev. iv. 5.
[71] Rev. viii. 3.
[72] Rev. v. 9-12.

RITUAL.

When to Thy beloved on Patmos
    Through the open door in Heaven,
Visions of the perfect worship,
    Saviour! by Thy love were given,
Surely *there* was truth and spirit,
    Surely there a pattern shown
How Thy Church should do her service
    When she came before the Throne.

O the censer-bearing Elders,
    Crowned with gold and robed in white!
O the Living Creatures' anthem,
    Never resting day or night!
And the thousand choirs of Angels,
    With their voices like the sea,
Singing praise to God the Father,
    And, O Victim Lamb, to Thee!

'Tis for Thee we bid the frontal
    Its embroidered wealth unfold,
'Tis for Thee we deck the reredos
    With the colours and the gold;
Thine the floral glow and fragrance,
    Thine the vesture's fair array,
Thine the starry lights that glitter
    Where Thou dost Thy Light display.

Lord, bring home the glorious lesson
    To their hearts, who strangely deem
That an unmajestic worship
    Doth Thy Majesty beseem;
Show them more of Thy dear Presence,
    Let them, let them come to know
That our King is throned among us,
    And His Church is Heaven below.

BOOKS CONSULTED AND REFERRED TO IN
CHAPTER II.

The Acts of the Apostles. Ragg and Rackham.
Letters of St. Ignatius. Lightfoot.
The Apostolic Fathers. Wake.
Epistles of St. Clement. Lightfoot.
Irenaeus, Oxford Edition.
Tertullian, Oxford Edition.
Eusebius, *History.*
Sozomen, *History.*
Age of the Fathers. Bright.
Apostolic Fathers. Burton.
Patristic Study. Prof. Swete.
Voice of the Fathers. Caulfield.
The City of God. St. Augustine.

CHAPTER III.

THE CHURCH IN BRITAIN.

WE DO NOT know at what time, or by whom, Christianity was introduced into Britain, any more than we know who carried it to Rome. Doubtless as the disciples were dispersed by persecution and went hither and thither, they told of Christ and proclaimed the Gospel.

There is a beautiful legend of St. Joseph of Arimathæa, who was banished from Palestine by the Jews, and who, with twelve companions, came to Britain, bringing with him the Holy Grail. He preached in the Isle of Avalon, where in confirmation of his teaching, he stuck his staff of thorn into the ground, whereupon it blossomed like Aaron's rod, and grew into a tree. Here the famous church and monastery of Glastonbury were founded. There is another story that[1] Lucius, the British King, sent to Eleuthereus, Bishop of Rome, a letter expressing a desire to be a Christian. This statement has been traced to a fabrication in Rome in the fifth century. For lack of authority, the story has led modern historians to reject it.[2] The Abbé Duchesne says: "This legend had a Roman, not a British, origin, and may probably have been invented in the fifth century." There is also a Welsh legend about Bran the Blessed, found in the Welsh Triads, collected in the thirteenth century. It relates how Bran, the father of Caractacus, having been detained by the Emperor Claudius for seven years at Rome, as a hostage for his son, was there converted by St. Paul, and on his release carried the faith back to Britain, and planted the Church there.[3] Oddly enough, the idea that St. Peter came to Britain has cropped up many times, and in widely different places, an error probably owing to a misapprehension of the fact of the sending of the monk St. Augustine to England by Pope Gregory. This view has even been put forth by a Roman Catholic clergyman of our own day. We

---

[1] Hore, *Hist. Ch. Eng.*, p. 3.
[2] Bright, *Early Eng. Ch. Hist.*, p. 4.
[3] Cutts, *Hist. Eng. Ch.*, p. 6.

have to be ever on our guard against accepting like untrustworthy legends for, as Professor Collins says,[4] "when there was a demand in the Middle Ages for any conceivable information on any conceivable subject, there was always some one ready to supply it." However controversialists may have adopted any of these stories, truth bids us not to use them.

The Account of St. Paul.

The account of St. Paul visiting Britain has more probability attached to it. Caractacus, the noble British Chief, had been pardoned, and sent by Rome back to his native country to rule over his tribe as a Roman official. His father Bran, and his son and daughter Lyn and Claudia, were retained in Rome as hostages. They were there at the same time St. Paul was there in residence. He lived in his own hired house, and made converts among Cæsar's household.

In his Epistle to the Romans, St. Paul makes mention of Linus, Pudens, and Claudia. Is not Linus the same as Lyn? A Claudia is commemorated by the historian Martial as married to Pu-

---

[4] Collins, *Eng. Christianity*, 43.

dens, the son of a Roman senator. It would seem therefore that the Linus and Claudia, mentioned as his converts by St. Paul, were the children of the British chief. Now it is a fair inference, indeed a certain one, that Lyn and Claudia would urge St. Paul to visit Britain and preach the Gospel to their own people. Certainly, St. Paul would have regarded this as a providential opening, and a call from God. The commission he had received from Christ and the Apostles ran to all the Gentile world. As he was on his way to Spain, why should he not extend his journey to Britain? Lightfoot, in his commentary on the Epistle to the Galatians, says St. Paul probably went to Gaul. It would be easy for him then to cross over to Britain. This theory has for its corroboration the statement of St. Clement that "St. Paul is said to have come to the boundary of the West," or, as it is otherwise translated, "furthest limits of the West." Now Spain was not a boundary of the Roman Empire, but Britain was.[5] The expression "furthest limits of the West," is a phrase which in Roman literature of the time was understood to include Britain.

---

[5] Lane's *Illus. Ch. His.*, p. 6.

We may agree with Dr. Bright and Professor Collins in holding St. Paul's visit not to be an ascertained historical fact, but yet hold it to be one of considerable probability. It seems like unto that of St. Peter's residence at Rome. Our Lord did not bid blessed Peter go to Rome, as he did St. Paul. There is no explicit statement in Scripture that he was ever there. There is no contemporary witness to the fact. There is no clear statement of St. Peter, nothing in contemporary history to confirm it. There is the tradition that he was martyred there, and upon this it is claimed that his body was buried there. So we may accept his having been there as a probable event. It is not, however, an ascertained historical fact, upon which a dogma can rightly be based.

In like manner, may we not hold as probable that St. Paul visited Britain? May we not believe with Irenæus, who was born in 97, that the Church was extended "by the Apostles to the utmost bounds of the West, and to the Celts"? Gildas, the British historian, after describing the defeat of Boadicea in 61, wrote: "In the meantime, Christ the true Sun, for the first time cast His rays on this island." Eusebius, in his history, says:

"Apostles crossed the ocean to those islands which are called British." Charles Butler, a Roman Catholic wrote: "It is probable that Christianity was disseminated over parts of Britain during the Apostolic age." Hore, a notable scholar, in summing up the authorities, says: "There can be no reasonable ground for doubting that the British Church was not only a very ancient one, but also of Apostolic foundation."

The Planting of Christianity.

It is regarded as probable that either in the Apostolic or sub-Apostolic age, Christianity had entered into Britain. It was certainly there in organized form, by the latter part of the second century. It came, not from Rome, but from Gaul. "In the reign of Marcus Aurelius, about 170, a mission consisting of Bishop Pothinus and a presbyter, Irenæus, a pupil of St. Polycarp, who had been a pupil of St. John, left Asia Minor. Sailing along the Mediterranean, they came to Marseilles and thence up the Rhone to the middle of Gaul. There at Vienne, near Lyons, they founded a church. From thence Christianity went,

---
[6] Hore, *Eighteen Centuries*.

perhaps pushed by persecution, further north, until finally missionaries crossed the Channel and planted the Church in Britain."[7] Not only is Christianity thus early found in Britain, but it is in its organized form of Episcopal government. The proof of this is that we have the names of three Bishops of Britain who attended the great Council of Arles, called in the year 314 to pass on the Donatist heresy. The records of this Council give the names of these three British Bishops who attended, Eborius of York, Restitutus of London, and Adelphius, Bishop of Colonia Londinensium (probably from Caerleon, Wales). These were accompanied by a presbyter, Sacerdos, and a deacon, Arminius.[8] This fact shows that by the beginning of the fourth century, the Church was established in Britain as far north as York, and probably as far west as Caerleon; that it had a diocesan Episcopate, and the three orders of the ministry; that it was in communion with other churches of the Empire; and that it was of sufficient importance to be summoned to a great and important Council. Later on also, in 359, we find

---
[7] Cutts' *Hist. Ch. Eng.*, p. 30.
[8] Hore, *Ch. of Eng.*; Cutts' *Eng. Ch. History*, p. 14.

British Bishops taking part in the Council of Ariminum. The poverty of these Bishops is expressly mentioned by Sulpicius Severus, who bears witness to the existence and temporal condition of their church.

There are also many subordinate evidences of an early existence of the Church in Britain. The remains of an early church building have been discovered at Silchester. Fragments of pottery with the holy sign have been upturned, a coin bearing the Alpha and Omega, and grave-stones with the inscription "a Christian sleeps below," have been found.[9] The Church came, as we have seen, from Gaul, not from Rome or directly from an Eastern source.

In 410, a great political event happened. The capture of Rome by Alaric shook the foundations of civilization. "To St. Jerome, in his cell at Bethlehem, the news came like the shock of an earthquake." He says, "My voice falters, sobs stifle the words I dictate; for she is a captive, that city which outrivalled the world." To St. Augustine, it was the judgment of God upon "the profligate manners, the effeminacy, and the pride of her

---

[9] Bright's *Early Ch. His.,* p. 11.

MARTYRDOM OF ST. ALBAN.

citizens." The Roman government was forced, for its own self protection, to withdraw its garrison from Britain, where they had been for nigh four hundred years. The Romans had done much there for civilization, and somewhat for Christianity. Converts had been made, and churches had grown up about their settlements. The literary remains are scanty of this time, but two interesting incidents relating to this period are commonly stated by historians. One of them is of the ennobling heroism of Britain's first martyr, St. Alban. While Alban was still a heathen, we read that one day there came to his house a priest, to whom Alban gave shelter from his persecutors. Alban saw that the stranger was very devout and holy, and marked his spending many hours in prayer. He opened the Gospel to Alban, and led him to believe in our Lord Jesus Christ. But at last the hiding place of the priest was discovered, and the soldiers came and surrounded it. St. Alban, perceiving the danger, dressed himself in the priest's clothes, so that the soldiers, breaking in, and seeing him in the habit of a priest, seized him and dragged him before the Judge. With fearless courage, Alban declared that he was a Christian. Though he was tortured to make him deny the Faith, he remained faithful, and was led out to execution. The soldier whose duty it was to execute him was so struck by Alban's splendid courage that, throwing away his sword, he declared himself also a Christian. It was an instance of the extension of the Faith from one brave heart to another by the power of the Spirit. The great Abbey of St. Albans, lately restored, is a memorial of the heroic devotion of these early Christians. The other instance is that of the Alleluia Battle. In the early days of the fifth century, a momentous theological controversy arose. Pelagius, whose Celtic name was Morgan, went astray by over-rating the power of the human will and denying the necessity of internal grace. The heresy, as all rationalistic speculations are, was attractive to some of the laity. Britain naturally made an appeal to her Mother Church of Gaul for aid in the controversy. The Gallican Church, we read, summoned a synod, which sent to the aid of the Church in Britain two of her greatest Bishops, Germanus and Lupus.[10] The authority for this statement is found in the life of St. Germanus,

---

[10] Bright's *Early Eng. Ch. Hist.*, pp. 15, 16.

THE AMERICAN CATHOLIC CHURCH. 55

by Constantius of Lyons, who wrote some sixty years after the decease of St. Germanus, with full access to local information. With respect to this controversy Constantius gives as his authority the action of the synod. His account is copied by the Venerable Bede, who states that the prelates, Germanus of Auxerre and Lupus of Troyes, were sent over by a synod to uphold in Britain the belief in Divine Grace." Prosper, another writer, says that Germanus was sent by the Bishop of Rome. But properly the official record of the synod is to be taken as a more reliable evidence than the unsupported and probably hearsay report recorded by Prosper. Possibly the Pope might have sent his blessing to Germanus, but the fact remains that the British Church in its need appealed to Gaul, and not to Rome. This was about the year 429. We are told that at a conference between the Pelagians and the Gallican Bishops, the Gallic party triumphed. After this, the invasion of Picts and Scots followed.

We now come to the Alleluia battle. Germanus and Lupus, the Gallic Bishops, encouraged the Britons to resist the invaders. They preached the

---

[11] Cutts' *Eng. Turning Points,* p. 16.

Gospel and brought a large number to Christ and to baptism. Here we quote largely from Professor Bright: "On Easter Eve, the baptisms were administered, the great Feast was celebrated in a church formed out of the boughs of trees, the British host advanced to the battle, the greater part of it fresh from the laver. Their general drew them up as if in ambush, under the rocks of a narrow glen which he had ascertained to lie full in the path of the enemy. As the first ranks of the heathen drew near, expecting an easy triumph, Germanus made the British people shout after him the one sacred joyous word, which they had so lately uttered in their paschal solemnities. Three times he and Lupus intoned it, Alleluia, Alleluia, Alleluia. Their followers with one voice made the sound echo through the valley. It rang from cliff to cliff. It struck the invaders with panic. They fled as if the very skies were crashing over them. The Britons, successful without striking a blow, exulted in a victory won by faith, without bloodshed." This is the story of the great Alleluia victory.

On the withdrawal of the Romans, the Britons, who had been originally disarmed by their conquerors, and thus rendered unaccustomed to warfare, were left practically defenceless. The country was left open to a great invasion of Jutes, Angles, and Saxons, coming from different parts of the continent. The three are commonly spoken of as Anglo-Saxons. The first work of the new invaders was to stamp out with fire and sword every trace of Roman civilization. "They seemed," says Professor Rollinston, "to have a great aptness for destroying and great slowness in elaborating material civilization." [12] These heathen Anglo-Saxons, we read, drove away or enslaved the Romanized and Christianized Celts, broke down every vestige of Christian civilization, destroyed the churches, burnt the villas, laid waste many of the towns, and reintroduced a long period of pagan barbarism. We quote from Grant Allen:[13] "These Anglo-Saxons were a horde of barbarous heathen pirates. They massacred or enslaved half the civilized Celtic inhabitants with savage ruthlessness. They let the roads and cities fall into utter disrepair. They stamped out Christianity with fire and sword from end to end of their new domain." As Gildas the historian, with Celtic fervor, phrases it: "The

---

[12] *Anglo-Saxon Britain*, Allen, p. 25.
[13] *Anglo-Saxon Britain*, Allen, p. 46.

red tongue of flame licked up the whole land from end to end, till it slaked its horrid thirst in the western ocean." There is however a difference among scholars to-day as to the extent of the Saxon destructions. The remains lately found go to show it was not so complete an extermination as has been represented by some historians. The Church, though enfeebled, continued to exist.

The Scotic Church.

When we look to the Scotic Church, we find it existing in an early period of the fourth century. Here came St. Ninian, about 397, and "preached the word to the southern Picts." The work was developed under St. Kentigern, and St. Columba in the latter half of the sixth century. The latter, having done much in Ireland, desired to "sojourn abroad for Christ's sake," and at Whitsuntide, 563, settled at Iona, and there founded that famous missionary monastery. "He was," says Adamnan, "angelic in aspect, clear in speech, holy in conduct, great in counsel; never did a single hour pass in which he was not engaged in prayer or pious work." "He was," writes Bright, "a grand saint, and a man of extraordinary courage, perseverance,

ST. COLUMBA AT ORONSAY. A.D. 563.

energy, and determination, born to guide minds and also to win hearts." Most have heard the story of his passing when the old monastic horse thrust his head into Columba's bosom, and the old monk said, "Let him alone, he loves me." His dying suggestion to his monks was to mutual charity: "But you who must rule after me; remember no deed can last, but only Love."

Native British Church.

At the dawning of the fifth century, the whole of the west coast of England, Cornwall, Wales, Cumberland, from Land's End to the Clyde, was being covered by the native British Church. "At this period," says Dr. Bright, "the headquarters of the British Church was Wales." In the middle of the sixth century, a religious revival took place. The Welsh Episcopacy then became regularly diocesan. It had its yearly synods, but it had no Metropolitan. It is of interest to observe how David, commonly known as St. David, when travelling in the Holy Land, in the sixth century, was there consecrated by the Patriarch of Jerusalem. He became the Archbishop of the See of St. David's, which subsequently was named after him.

In the year 1115 the Welsh Bishops became united with the English Church, under the Archbishop of Canterbury. Eventually the Bishop of Landaff, a successor in this line, united with Laud in his consecrations and thus passed on the ancient British succession from the Patriarch of Jerusalem.

The Celtic Church.

The planting of Christianity in Ireland is obscure. It was carried there probably by Christians from Britain. Palladius, in 431, is spoken of as the first Bishop of the Irish, but he is reported as practically failing in his work. The great name that looms up before us is that of St. Patrick. So many legends have surrounded his life that it is difficult to know what is true. The only reliable sources are a book of Confessions written by him, and some prayers, or hymns. He was of British parentage, his father or grandfather being a clergyman. When a lad, with others, he was stolen and carried away to Ireland. He became a shepherd, and while looking after his sheep, he was drawn to meditation, and "he remembered his own sins and was converted." A strong desire filled his soul to serve Christ. Escaping from his captivity, he found his way back to his home and native land. But having a call, as he believed, from God, he went back to Ireland, and being ordained, became its missionary. He does not tell us who ordained him. His success is probably exaggerated. Along with St. Patrick, the name of St. Columbanus is prominent. There is no more typical Irish missionary. Bright calls him a "pious, fearless, self-devoted man, with not a little of Celtic passion in his nature." Having addressed Pope Boniface as "head of all the Churches of Europe, and Pastor of pastors," he nevertheless lectured him as having appeared to compromise the faith.

One mark of the old Irish Church was its love of teaching and study. Bede remarks upon the open-hearted, generous hospitality extended to Anglican students attracted to Ireland by the fame of its monastic schools. What the old Irish Church lacked conspicuously was organization. The Episcopal character was bestowed very freely on priests, and the monasteries were ruled over by Abbot-Bishops. A tribal influence affected the Church, and Bishops were often members of some particular family within the tribe. It was at the Synod of Kells that Ireland gained its first hierarchical organization, with four provinces having four Archbishops, a primacy being reserved to Armagh.

It may be noted that the line of Bishops from St. Patrick extended down to the Reformation, when some of the Irish Bishops, whose consecration has never been questioned, conformed to the Anglican Church in the time of Queen Elizabeth, and imparted to Archbishop Laud the Episcopal order. The gradual rechristianizing of the major part of Britain, which came to be called the Heptarchy, we will treat of in a following chapter.

THE CHARACTER OF THE CHURCH.

We come now to a question which has involved some dissension. The ordinary lay reader will be perhaps perplexed by the different estimates put by writers upon the character and standing of the British Celtic Churches. This, we are sorry to say, has come about through the controversial spirit which has influenced the different writers. There is a strong inclination amongst some to magnify the work of the monk Augustine, sent by Pope Gregory in the sixth century, and thus to give to our Anglican Church a Roman origin. There are others who look to the ancient British and Celtic Churches as ancestral parts of our own Communion, and who are led therefore, perhaps, to emphasize their Catholic character and position. Justice and truth, however, bid us hold the scales evenly balanced, and not let our judgment be carried away by partisan prepossessions. The indictment against the British Church, made with considerable heat, is that "the Church was weak, confined to the Roman provinces; and had no strength or character of its own, but was a reflection of its Gallic sister." "It produced," it is said, "no writers or scholars. It was lacking in a missionary spirit. It looked to Gaul for the saints it would follow and reverence. It was poor, too poor to endow even its own Bishops. It founded no school of theology. It was monastic, and therefore ascetic rather than evangelical." Gildas the historian, about 564, found fault with the Church, but "made his attack," says Dr. Bright, "in so unbalanced and vehement a manner that it provokes incredulity by its very violence." "His description," writes Professor Zimmer, "is no matter-of-fact account of the British Church, but rather the penitential sermon of a man who delights to paint everything in the blackest colors."

In considering the charge of want of aggressiveness preferred against the early British Church, it must be remembered that the Church labored under great difficulties. She had an internal racial dissension to contend with between the Goidels and the Bythens, two different races inhabiting Britain. The Church also suffered terribly from the invasions of her heathen conquerors. Its members were driven largely into the mountainous country of Cornwall, Wales, and Cumberland, and were necessarily scattered. The Church was indeed very poor. No wonder she did not do an aggressive work amongst the Saxons. The Saxon conquerors were not disposed to accept for teachers a hated race.

To the charge that the Church had no great scholars we would reply that the lack of scholars is no sign of decadence. St. Paul bids St. Timothy entrust the work and government of the Church to *faithful* men. Scholarship is apt to bring with it a danger. It gives rise to controversies and heresies. It is far better for a Church to be orthodox and faithful than to be noted for its scholarship; and the British and Celtic Churches had the reputation of orthodoxy. St. Chrysostom bears witness to her unity in the Faith. He says of Britain, "There, too, as in the extreme East, beside the Euxine Sea, in the South, even, men may be heard discoursing words of Scripture, in differing tongues, but not with differing beliefs."

"Britain," says St. Jerome, "worships the same Christ, observes the same rule of Faith, as other Christian countries." Wilfred, who was Roman in his sympathies, asserted that the true Catholic Faith was held by the Irish, the Scottish, and the British, as well as by the Anglo-Saxon Church. In regard to its relation to Europe, Dr. Bright says, "We find it adhering to orthodox doctrine during the great Arian struggle." Hilary of Poitiers, in 358, congratulated his British brethren on their "freedom from all contagion of this detestable heresy." In 363 Athanasius could reckon the Britons amongst those loyal to the Catholic Faith.[14] We have also seen how, with the help of brethren from Gaul, the Celtic Church stemmed the Pelagian heresy. Both the British and Celtic Churches were equally free from the negations of modern Protestantism and the modern additions of Rome. In other words she was *orthodox*.

---

[14] Bright's *English Ch.*, 12.

The existence of the many monasteries proves also that the Church had a sincere devotional side. Though the monastic system has been found fault with for being ascetic, yet its counsels of poverty, chastity, and obedience were given by our Blessed Lord Himself, who in His own Person was the best Exemplar of them. The monk took up his life as a follower of Jesus Christ. It was a life of labor and of prayer. The good monk, perhaps better than any other man, followed the example of the Lord. He became spiritually a man of God, singularly united to Christ by the power of the Holy Ghost. The world looks on, and may approve of the good work he does, but its enfeebled sight does not discern the supernatural spirituality and power of the consecrated life. The existence and development of the many monasteries in Britain at this time bear witness to the life of devotion in the early British Church, which at least equals the devotion of the unpersecuted, comfortable Christianity of the present day.

The prevalence of the monasteries all over the country greatly aided the extension of Christianity. They abounded in good works. "Secure in the peace conferred upon them by religious sanction,

IONA AT THE PRESENT DAY.

the monks became the builders of schools, the clearers of forests, the tillers of heath." "The reclaiming of the waste land about the marshes," says Grant Allen, in his work on ancient Britain, "was almost entirely due to monastic bodies. The monks were agriculturists, masons, jewellers, glass-blowers, and scribes. The monasteries became real manufacturing, agricultural, and literary centres. The monks copied illuminated manuscripts, and painted pictures, not without rude merit." In the Irish monasteries we find them presided over by Abbots in Episcopal orders. "The spread of Christianity," says Professor Collins, "lay in the formation of monastic societies; and this is the strongest possible evidence of the essential character of an apostolically descended ministry carefully guarded." The spirit of unworldliness and devotion to Christ and the purity and fervour of these early monks must have left their stamp on the whole Church of this period. The British and Celtic Churches, we conclude, were orthodox in Faith, Apostolic in government, and evangelical in spirit.

While the British Church established itself in the West, gradually the rest of England was reconverted, and there arose what we might call the Anglo-Saxon or Celtic Church. The story of its conversion we shall state subsequently.

Relation of the Church to Rome.

What, we may ask, was the relation of the British and Celtic Churches to Rome at this time? They were independent of Rome. Britons undoubtedly looked to Rome as the great capital of the Empire, and to the Bishop there as the first in Christendom. St. Columbanus speaks of him as the "Head of the Western Church," or of the whole Church. He also gives him other titles, couched in warm and complimentary language.[15] But there is throughout the letters an implied assertion of exemption from Roman jurisdiction. Evidently he did not regard the pope as having monarchical powers or coercive jurisdiction, or as endowed with a gift of infallibility; for the saint does not hesitate to warn the Bishop of Rome of the "dreadful scandal and calamity it would be to the Church if he were to fall into error." He implies thus the possibility of his doing so. He would surely have repudiated the reported utter-

---

[15] Warren's *Celtic Lit.*, p. 38.

ance of Pope Pius IX., April 1, 1886, "I am the Way, the Truth, and the Life." "They who are with me are with the Church, and they who are not with me are out of the Church."

The Celtic Church, as had been the British, was *free from Roman dominion*. The case of Wilfrid is one proof of this. Theodore (664) the Archbishop of Canterbury, had divided the large See of York. Wilfrid, the Archbishop of York, appealed to Rome. Rome decided in favor of Wilfrid that he should be reinstated in the undivided See. But Archbishop Theodore ignored the Papal authority and refused to have Wilfrid reinstated. The great body of the clergy and laity did not stand with Wilfrid. "To all," says Dr. Bright, "the See of Peter was a title of august and sacred import. But they had not as a body, in 678, any notion that gratitude or reverence could bind them to recognize a systematic interference on the part of Rome in their domestic Church matters, by virtue of which any national Church decision might at any time be nullified by a court of appeal sitting beyond the Alps." The aversion to "outlandish" authority rendered them scornfully incredulous as to the practical exercise of any such power.

It is not by the sayings of any, even of saints, that the relation between the Church and Rome is to be known. It can only be determined by the solid evidence of ascertained facts. The Church stood towards Rome on the same equality as did the Continental Churches. It is said that St. Patrick had a canon passed in the Irish Church providing in certain cases for an appeal to Rome. But this St. Patrick legend is an untrustworthy one, and Stubbs and Haddon question the genuineness of this canon. Moreover, Britain was not controlled by the papacy, for the powers now exercised by the papacy were then unknown anywhere.[16] The legal opinion of Blackstone is clear and decided. "The ancient British Church, by whomsoever planted, was a stranger to Rome and all its pretended authority." [17]

This is proved by the fact that the Bishops of the British Church were not chosen by the Pope, but she selected and consecrated them; nor were they required to take their jurisdiction from Rome.

---

[16] Collins' *Eng. Christianity*, p. 21.
[17] Blackstone, *Com. IV.*, ch. viii.

The Pope could neither appoint nor remove a Bishop at his own discretion, as he now claims the right to do. The Archbishop of the Britons was of their own choice. He was not obliged to receive from Rome the pall, which was in early times a gift of honor when conferred. Down to the time of Gregory it was considered nothing more than an honorary and complimentary badge.[18] All executive, legislative, and administrative powers were not, as today, centred in the papacy.

The idea of subjection to any other Bishop or Church than the one of Britain would have been quite absurd to the British Christians. The name of Holy Jerusalem or of great Rome might be spoken of with high honor, but that was all. Anything more would have been foreign to their whole mode of thought. That this was so, comes out very emphatically when Augustine demanded the submission of the British Bishops to himself. They positively rejected his claims, declaring allegiance to an Archbishop of their own, the Bishop of Caerleon-upon-Usk. "Be it known unto you," they said, "we are subject to the Church of God, and to the Pope of Rome, and to every godly

---

[18] Cutts' *Augustine of Canterbury*, Ch. xiii.

Christian to love every one. But other obedience than this we do not know due to him whom you name to be Pope." This, we think, is sufficient to settle the question of their relation to the papacy. Warren sums the situation as follows: "There was a vast Celtic communion existing in Great Britain and Ireland, sending its missions among Teutonic tribes on the Continent, and to distant islands like Iceland; Catholic in doctrine and practice, with a long roll of saints, every one of note named among them, like St. Columbanus, taking a line wholly independent of Rome, or like Bishop Colman at the Synod of Whitby directly in collision with her, a communion having its own Liturgy, its own translation of the Bible, its own mode of chanting, its own monastic rule, its own cycle for the calculation of Easter, and presenting both internal and external evidence of complete autonomy" [19]

The Celtic Liturgy.

It will now be interesting to learn what were the Liturgy and customs of the Celtic Church at this time; how in some respects she differed from the other branches of the Catholic Church, and yet

---

[19] Warren's *Cel. Ch. Lit.*, p. 45.

in the essential points was the same; and how we, her sons and daughters, in these modern times, can be sure our Liturgy resembles that of the Celtic period in its first purity and freshness. We gather the following from Warren, the learned writer on Celtic Liturgy: "In many respects, the Celtic Church conformed to the liturgy of the neighboring country of Gaul, which had received its forms of worship from the East. There were churches, we learn, with bells, and altars of wood or stone. Their liturgy or altar service was known by the name of *"communion eucharistua," "hostia, oblatio, sacrificium, beaticum."* The Lord's Prayer was an essential part of the service, and it is to be noted that in our Anglican Church no service can be said without it. There were proper prefaces as with us, and to pray for the dead was a recognized custom. According to the Apostolic custom, the kiss of peace was given after the prayer of consecration. The services both at the altar and in the choir were choral. In Ireland, music was an art early cultivated. In the ancient Irish Church, a hymn was sung after the prayer of consecration. Unleavened bread was used. Dr. Döllinger mentions the use of unleavened bread in the Eucharist among the peculiarities of the ancient British Church. The universal custom of the primitive Church to mix a little water with the wine in the Eucharistic cup obtained in the Celtic Church also. "Frequent mention is made of the use of the sign of the Cross for various purposes." That was the sign ordinarily attending the sacerdotal act of benediction. Special vestments were in use at the altar. Among them we find noted the chasuble, the alb, and the maniple. Among the Bishop's ornaments were a ring, a pectoral cross, and a pastoral staff. The position of the celebrant was before the altar, and with his back to the congregation. The communion hymn of the early Irish Church is full of allusions to the reception of the chalice. The act of communion was called, in the rule of the Irish Culdees, "going to the chalice." There were differences between the British Church and the Roman, as we have said, in respect to the celebration of the time for Easter. There was some difference also in respect to the administration of baptism, the wearing of the tonsure, the use of different selections of Scripture in the Ordinal, and the anointing of the hands of deacons and priests in ordination.

Thus in doctrine and worship, we see that the Celtic Church in Britain conformed in all essentials to Holy Scripture and the teaching of Apostolic times, while in several respects it varied from the Roman practice. The Celtic Church was poor and not aggressive. It had been driven into a state of isolation. It had suffered from cruel wars. It had, however, kept the Faith, the Apostolic government, the Priesthood, and it offered a true worship and was kept alive in God's great Providence. We may well look to her as our spiritual Mother, with a grateful heart, and be thankful that we have inherited so much from her whose daughters we are.

BOOKS REFERRED TO IN CHAPTER III.

Early English Church. Bright.
History of the English Church. Hunt.
Roman Britain. E. Conybeare.
Celtic Britain. J. Rhys.
The Celtic Church. Zimmer.
Sketches of Church History. Robertson.
Anglo-Saxon Britain. Grant Allen.
How the Church came to England. Gertrude Hollis.
Theodore and Wilfrid. Rt. Rev. Dr. Browne.
History of the Church, A. D. 313-451. Bright.
The Early English Church. Churton.
Ecclesiastical History. Bede.
Our Island Church. Douglas Macleane.
Story of Ireland and Her Church. Macbeth.

Turning Points of English Church History. Cutts.
Beginnings of English Christianity. Collins.
Conversion of the Heptarchy. Bishop Browne.
Life of St. Columba. Ed. A. Cooke.

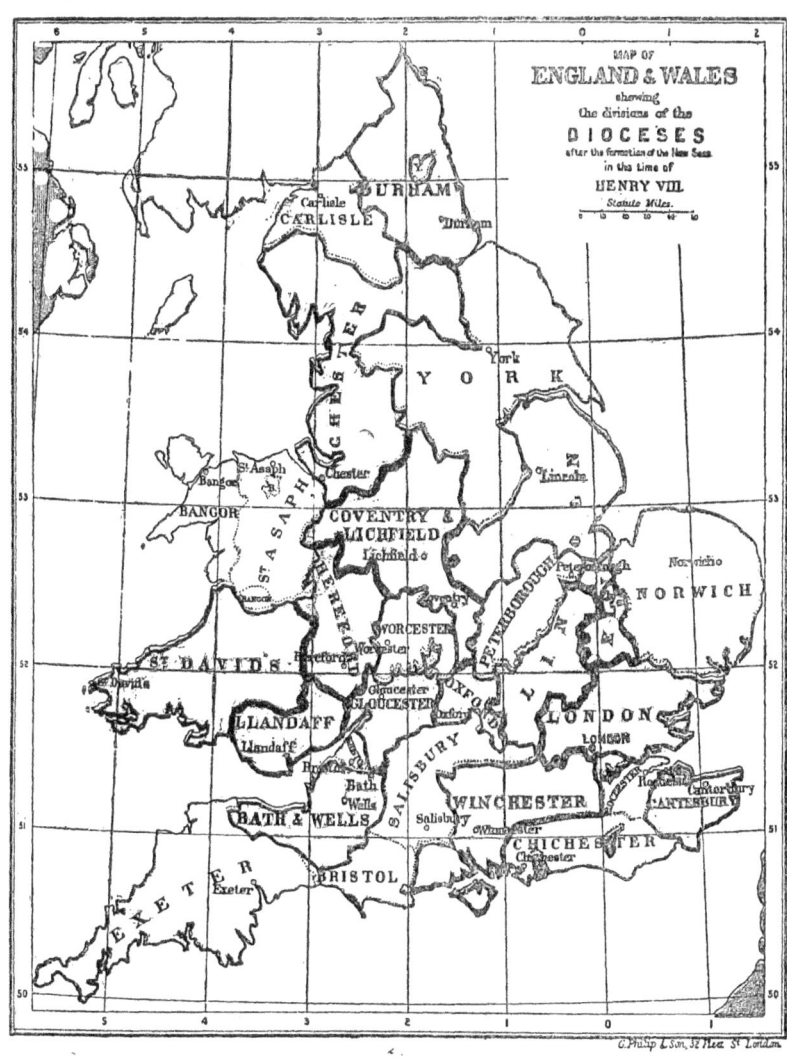

CHAPTER IV.

FORMATION OF THE CHURCH OF ENGLAND.

GRADUALLY the territory of the heathen invaders who were continually fighting with one another became consolidated at the end of the sixth century into seven kingdoms called the Heptarchy. These were Northumbria, Mercia, East Saxons, West Saxons or Wessex, East Anglia, South Saxons, Kent. The work of planting Christianity in these seven kingdoms had to begin practically anew. It is to be observed, however, that the old British Church that had fled westward had little to do with this missionary work. It had to be done by others. There were three sources from which devoted missionaries came: from the north, and from the west, and from the continent. Among these we have St. Patrick, Columbanus, Aidan, Augustine, and Paulinus.

We will begin the story with the large northeastern kingdom of Northumbria. Paulinus, Queen Ethelburga's chaplain, obtained permission from King Edwin, who was a heathen, to hold a general conference, in which Paulinus should be allowed to present the claims of the Gospel. There is an interesting account of what occurred. An old chief arose and summed up the issue between the rival faiths in a striking manner. "I will tell you, O King, what methinks man's life is like. Sometimes when your hall is lit up for supper on a wild winter's evening, and warmed by a fire in the midst, a sparrow flies in by one door, takes shelter for a little time in the warmth, and then flies out again by another door, and is lost in the stormy darkness. No one in the hall sees the bird before it enters or after it is gone forth, and it is only seen for a little time as it hovers near the blazing hearth. Even so is it, I ween, as to this brief span of our life in this world. What has gone before, what will come after it, of this we know nothing. If the strange teacher can tell us, by all means let him be heard."[1] This decided the question with the assembly. The pagan high priest himself led the way, and with his own hand desecrated the heathen temple. It was the birthday of the Northumbrian Church.

[1] *Early Eng. Ch.*, Bright, p. 116. *Title-deeds Eng. Ch.*, Garnier, p. 44.

Then King Penda, a fierce heathen and savage warrior, overthrew the Northumbrians, and Christianity was all but swept away. It was subsequently reconquered by the Britons, and was ruled over by a Christian British king, representing the Christianity of the old British Church. Oswald, the king, had in 635, in his desire to Christianize his people, sent to a monastery in Iona for a Bishop. The Bishop, however, soon returned from Northumbria, and reported that "He could make nothing of the British. They were hard, untractable, barbarous." The monk Aidan observed that "the Bishop appeared to have expected too much at first. It would have been better," he observed, "to have obeyed the Apostolic precept, 'Treat them as infants in the Faith, and feed them with the milk of easier doctrine.'"[2] "He might," says Bishop Browne of Bristol, "have been telling us in our day how to deal with some of our people."

Aidan was seen by the Council to be the man for the task, and was consecrated. He did a very great and noble work. From him we may observe the present Bishops of Durham have succeeded,

---
[2] Bede, *Ecc. His.,* Book III., Ch. v.

ST. AIDAN PREACHING TO THE NORTHUMBRIANS. A.D. 635-642.

and now the eighty-fourth Bishop from Aidan sits in that See. Aidan's manner of life has thus been described by Bede: "He lived as he taught others to live. He neither sought nor loved this world's goods. He delighted in giving to the poor whatever the king and the great men gave to him. He moved about the country on foot, unless some real necessity compelled him. Whenever he saw wayfarers, he went to them at once. If they were unbelievers, he begged them to receive the Faith, and if they were believers, he strengthened them in the Faith, and urged them by word and deed to alms and good works."[3] It is related of him that when consulted by a certain priest, Utta, who asked his prayers for a journey, Aidan told him that he would meet with a tremendous storm on his return voyage, and he gave Utta a vessel of blessed oil, bidding him cast it on the waters when the storm came. It fell out as Aidan had said, and it stilled the raging of the storm. Aidan seems thus providentially to have been guided to a modern discovery.[4]

---

[3] Bede, *Eccl. His.*, Book III., Ch. v.
[4] *Conver. Hep.*, Bp. Browne, p. 107.

Professor Bright says of Aidan that "He set a pattern of ministerial activity, of absolute conspicuous unworldliness, of tenderness to the poor and weak, of boldness in behalf of right before the strong, of thorough-going, intense resolution to carry out in life the moral teaching of Scripture, which Bede, Latin as he was in tone, has described with a loving reverence." [5]

The English Church has always held Aidan in high regard, and looked upon him as one of the great missionaries through whom England received Christianity.

He observed the Scotic, or old British, rule for calculating his Easter, which rule was afterwards abandoned at the famous Synod of Whitby in 664, and the Continental custom adopted.

At Whitby we come across the Abbess Hilda and the beautiful story of the poet Caedmon. Hilda was a remarkable woman, noted both for her intellectual ability, administrative power, and sanctity. She was at the head of what were practically two monasteries, one of men and one of women. Upon them she impressed her own mind. They bowed to her as their head. She succeeded in es-

---

[5] Bright's *His. Early Eng. Ch.*, Ch. v.

tablishing a tradition of unanimity and unselfishness. She made her monks give so much time to the study of Scripture, and so much heed to the practice of good works, that Bishops came to think of her house as the best place for supplying competent ordinands. Five of the brethren, whom Bede enumerates as persons of signal worth and holiness, attained the Episcopal dignity.

There was one member of the monastery whom his brethren venerated for his specially inspired gift. Caedmon, for such was his name, was a poor and ignorant herdsman. He felt greatly humiliated that he was lacking in the power of song. One night he had a dream. A visitant stood by him, who said to him, "Caedmon, sing me something." "I cannot sing." "However, you have got to sing to me." "What must I sing?" "Sing the Creation." Solemn and adoring words came to his mind in rythmic measure. And when the morning came he was able to repeat them. The story came to the Abbess Hilda, who sent for him and tested his gift in various ways, by giving him other portions of Scripture in like manner to paraphrase. She took this poor ignorant herdsboy into the monastery and had him instructed in the Holy

Scriptures. Caedmon set everything by his gift to the music of song. Very sweetly, after years of loving service, he passed away. Knowing that his hour was drawing near, he asked for the Housel, or Sacrament. To the brethren present he said, "Are you kindly disposed towards me ?" "Surely, and we pray you to be so towards us." "Dear children," such is the sweet answer, "I am friendly disposed towards *all* God's servants." He then fortified himself with the heavenly viaticum, and fell asleep in Jesus.[6]

Next let us consider the Kingdom of West Saxony, or Wessex, in the south, which was founded by Cerdic about the year 519. It became eventually the most important of all the kingdoms of the Heptarchy. It gradually absorbed to itself all the others, and its kings became kings of England. In the times of which we speak Wessex had not become supreme. Ere it became supreme, it was exposed through various wars to fluctuations of territory. The knowledge of Christ came in the time of King Cynegils. Christianity in Wessex had, however, greatly suffered, and it had largely become pagan. About the year 633, a man named

---

[6] *Early Eng. Ch.*, Bright, p. 275.

Birinus was greatly drawn to preach the Gospel to the heathen in the unvisited parts of Britain. He applied to Pope Honorius, and was sent by him to be consecrated by Astorius, Bishop of Milan. He received from him what we should call a roving commission. He landed, probably, at Porchester in Wessex. He had come in search of a heathen people as yet unvisited by Christian missionaries. He found that the people of Wessex were mostly pagan. It was therefore unnecessary for him to proceed further in pursuance of his design. "He thought it more useful to remain there and preach the word than to go elsewhere." "It is important to notice that there is no hint that he thought it advisable to refer this complete change of plans to Rome." Though Honorius had befriended him, he had not come under any commission from Rome. So he began where he was: first, he taught King Cynegils the Christian creed, and baptized him. Now it was the office of the chief sponsor to receive the newly baptized Christian by giving him his hand as he emerged from the laver of regeneration. This office was performed by the most holy and most victorious King Oswald of Northumbria. Here, in a striking form, we have the Northum-

86   THE LINEAGE OF

brian influence in the conversion of a great Saxon kingdom, eventually the greatest of all. Kent (the home of the Roman mission), had already become divided, and was to divide still more. In the conversion of Wessex we lay our hand upon the Christianizing of the finally dominant kingdom. And while it was done by a Bishop designated from Italy, it was done in disregard of the original mission from Rome. Not only were there no relations between Birinus and the Canterbury or Roman Mission, but the one home influence there was in the conversion of Wessex was that of the most devoted adherent of the Scotic Church.

The people of Wessex, influenced by the King's example, were led to embrace Christianity in considerable numbers, and received Holy Baptism. Oswald, the King of Northumbria, coöperated in the establishment and development of the Church. The two kings built a church dedicated to St. Peter and St. Paul at Dorchester, near Oxford. Here Birinus settled himself. He built and dedicated churches; Bede tells us he won many people to the Lord by his pious labors; he died in 650. King Cynegils had passed away seven years previously. He was succeded by his son Coinwalch. He was a heathen, but after some trouble which involved his leaving his kingdom for a time, he became converted to Christianity. He looked round to find, after the death of Birinus, a Bishop for himself and his people. He was led to select Agilbert. Thus it was from the Scotic Church that the second line of Bishops came. Subsequently, as the king knew no other language, he brought in another Bishop named Wini, who spoke the same language as himself, and was consecrated in Gaul. Agilbert later withdrew, and went to Gaul, his native country, and became Bishop of Paris. He suggested his nephew Eleuthereus as his successor. Coinwalch applied to Theodore, then Archbishop of Canterbury, to consecrate him, and Theodore did so. We do not give the full details of these changes and nominations, but we insert two conclusions of Bishop Browne upon them. It is noticeable that these Bishops were not either elected by the people or clergy, or nominated from Rome, but were the direct appointees of the king. Nor is there any evidence to be found of the sway of Rome in England. "Coinwalch and Agilbert and Wini behaved as though they had never heard the name of Rome. They might perhaps have behaved better, if they had shown a sense of union and communion with the Patriarch of the West; and if the Patriarch of the West had imagined that it was at all his business, he might perhaps have kept them in better order. That does not touch the historical fact that Rome's hand was not felt in Wessex, indeed was not stretched out."

Wessex became Christianized, and from it early in the tenth century we have the Sees of Winchester, Cherbourne, Ramsbury, Wells, and Crediton. Later on were developed from it the sees of Exeter, Salisbury, and half of Gloucester and Bristol.

Coming to East Anglia, or Saxony, we find that King Redwald, during an absence from home, in Kent, embraced Christianity. His conversion however, was not very thorough. For on his return, meeting with the disapproval and opposition of his wife, he compromised his faith by erecting in his temple of worship two altars, one Christian and one heathen. His son Eorpwald, who succeeded him, was a pagan. So the temple remained with its double worship for many years.

It came about that in Redwald's lifetime, Edwin, King of Deira, had been driven from his kingdom by his brother-in-law, Ethelfrith the Ravager. He sought refuge at the Court of Redwald, who generously gave him hospitality. Three times the brother-in-law made offers of money, and each time larger, if he would put Edwin to death. Very wisely, he accompanied his last refusal by mobilizing an army. He did this so quickly that Ethelfrith was taken by surprise. In the battle that ensued he was slain, and also a son of Redwald's. This loss on his behalf strengthened the tie between Edwin and Redwald. When Edwin subsequently regained his throne, and became a Christian, he sought to repay Redwald's devotion and loss in his cause. After some years, Redwald being dead, out of gratitude to his memory, Edwin persuaded Eorpwald to abandon his heathenism and with his whole people to receive the Gospel and sacraments. Bede assigns this work of conversion wholly to Edwin.

After the death of Eorpwald, his brother Sigebert succeeded to the kingdom. Sigebert had been educated in France, and there became a Christian, and when he came to his kingdom he set himself to establish schools such as he had seen in his residence abroad. He was a man of devout life, and after reigning some years he retired to a monastery. His country being invaded, he was obliged to submit to his people's demands to fight for them. But refusing to be armed, he went into battle, Gordon-like, with a wand in his hand. Thus this most Christian and learned king fell in battle. He had been helped in his Christianizing work by a Bishop who came from Burgundy, by the happy name of Felix. Bede refers to the name, as if it had a sacramental meaning, and tells us that Felix brought pagans out of their long subjection to wickedness and unhappiness, and led them on to the Faith.[7] In the transept window of St. Paul's Cathedral, London, we find Sigebert placed among the Christian kings of the Heptarchy, and Felix among its twelve primary Bishops. Anna, who succeeded Sigebert, was quite as remarkable for Christian graces as Sigebert had been. The early Christianity of his reign was marked by two features, the presence in East Anglia of the Irish hermit Furzy and the dedication of Anna's daughters to the Religious life.

It is a grateful incident to recall that Felix was much helped in his missionary work by a

---

[7] Bede's *Ecc. His.,* Book II., Ch. 15.

monk whose name was Furzy. He belonged to a Scotic family, and came with a number of fellow-laborers from Ireland. He so won the people of Norfolk and Suffolk by his enthusiasm and Celtic eloquence that Christianity took a firmer hold among the people. This is the first recorded instance of union between the Celtic and the Continental teachers. We here quote from Professor Lane, as recording the spirit of the Churches: "The monks of Canterbury were sorely grieved when they heard of Felix working side by side with the representative of the British Church which they so despised, especially so as Furzy continued to wear the tonsure which they hated, and observe other customs of discipline and ritual in a different way to themselves. But, as they had no jurisdiction in East Anglia, they had to put up with the inconvenient reflections his undoubted success caused them. The Venerable Bede, who cannot be accused of too great affection for Celtic customs, has warmly praised Furzy's work, and testified to the numerous monasteries which the Irish monk had been instrumental in founding."[8] This testimony of Christian fellowship and co-

---

[8] Lane's *Illus. Eng. Ch. His.*, p. 65.

operation is a worthy example for our own days. "Even the keeping of Easter on different days was found to be not incompatible with fraternal sympathy, while holy Aidan lived at Lindisfarne. Although these were the ostensible subjects of controversy, the real sting in the quarrel was the broader question whether the ancient Church of Britain should give up its independence as an autonomous Church at the bidding of the Bishop of another Church; for no doubt had ever been cast in earlier times upon the right of the British Bishops to the claim of an independent origin." [9]

Another noted feature in East Anglia was the number of high-born women who gave themselves to the religious life. King Anna, who succeeded Sigebert, had a number of daughters who entered convents. It seems not to have been uncommon for ladies of high position to go over to France for their education. There they were brought in contact with nuns and religious life. Among Anna's daughters was Sexberga. She married the King of Kent; on being left a widow, she founded the convent of Minster, in the Isle of Sheppey. Afterwards she went to her sister Etheldreda's Abbey of

---

[9] Lane's *Illus. Ch. His.*, p. 78.

Ely, where in 679, she succeeded her sister as Abbess. Her own daughter followed her as Abbess of Ely, and another daughter as Abbess of Sheppey. The other daughters of King Anna were Witberga, an Ely nun, and Ethelberga. Ethelberga went for her education to Brie, near Meaux, in France. So great were her virtues, that in the course of time she was made Abbess. The same lot had previously fallen to King Anna's stepdaughter, Sæthryd. It was thus not uncommon in those days for great ladies to consecrate their lives in the Religious life. We have seen in the Celtic Church how much was due in Ireland and Britain to the monastic system. It was the backbone, or rather life blood, of the Church. Men and noble women were willing to give themselves and their all to Christ, who gave His All to them. Ah, would it were that in our day and our communion there might be many who would follow their noble example!

In the great central kingdom of Mercia the people were not Saxons or Jutes, but Angles. The most trying times in this struggle of the recovery of Christianity were the years from 633 to 655. In those years, Penda, a violent pagan, was King of Mercia. He did all he could to crush out Christianity. He had, however, a son, Pæda, described by Bede as "an excellent young man," to whom his father gave the kingdom of the Middle Angles. He married Elfleda, a Christian Princess. It is to be noted that there was a remarkable series of Christian princesses in a line of eight descents from mother to daughter, whose pagan husbands became Christian kings.[10]

Pæda was brought up a pagan. The condition proposed to him by Elfleda's father was that he might have her, provided he became a Christian. It is said that when he learned the promises of the Gospel and of the heavenly kingdom, he declared he would become a Christian, "wife or no wife." His companions and their dependents were baptized, and four priests were sent with Pæda to teach his people. These four missionaries preached to the middle Anglians with great success. "Every day people came to them, both nobles and those of lower degree, and renounced the vileness of idolatry and were washed clean in the font of faith." Not only among the middle Angles did they preach, but the murderous old pagan

---

[10] *Conversion of the Heptarchy*, Bp. Browne, 106-110.

Penda allowed them to do so to his Mercian subjects, if they wished to hear him. He had so far softened in his attitude towards Christianity that all he now demanded was that if any of his subjects became Christians they must become Christians in deed. He hated those who professed and called themselves Christians and did not obey the God in whom they believed. "I have always," says Bishop Browne, from whom we quote the above, "had a kindly feeling for this downright old pagan."[11]

In East Saxony, where London now is, were to be found the most perverse and determined pagans in the Seven Kingdoms. In 604 they received the Faith under Miletus their Bishop, whose seat was at London. His church was the forerunner of the present Cathedral of St. Paul, and the estate of Tillingham in Essex, which was given for its support, is held by the Cathedral chapter to-day.

From 650 to 653, London and the Kingdom of Essex remained pagan. It was not till a Saxon Bishop sat on the throne of Canterbury that London was brought once more to the Christian faith. Siegbert the King was a friend of the Christian King Oswi.

---

[11] *Conversion of the Heptarchy*, 110.

It is wise to remember on passing judgment on the question, what were the influences by which Britain was reconverted, and how much was due to missionaries from the North and West called the Scotic Bishops, and how much the influence came from the Roman Mission founded in 597 by the Mission of Augustine.

Bishop Browne states that two Scotic kings, Oswald and Oswi, with their Scotic Bishops, Igan and Finnon, were the converting and rechristianizing agents in Northumbria and Mercia, the East Saxon Kingdom, and Wessex. "Not even," says Bishop Browne,[12] "in the most direct way can any connection be traced with the Italian Mission, or any sort of reference to Canterbury or to Rome." "The Italian influence and the influence of Kent were entirely absent from the whole of the great domains of Northumbria and Mercia. The same was true of the whole of Wessex, the next largest portion of England, and also of Essex. In the year 655, sixty years after the arrival of the Italian mission, Northumbria, Mercia, East Saxony, and Wessex were all ruled by prelates of Irish or Scotic extraction. The teaching of Christianity

---

[12] *Conversion of the Heptarchy*, p. 113.

was entirely in the hands of men of the pre-Augustine churches of these islands, the Celtic and the Scotic Church."

We must now go back a little in time, and describe *The Italian Mission,* by the *Monk Augustine.*

It is a story as familiar to English youth as that of Washington and his hatchet is to Americans, but it is not so universally known among Churchmen in the United States.

About the year 595, we come to the story of the famous mission of Augustine. Gregory—an Abbot at that time of the monastery on the Cœlian Hill at Rome—was passing through the Forum, when he observed a group of slaves who were exposed there for sale. In contrast with the brown skins, black hair, and dark eyes of the Italians, the fair complexions and blue eyes of the Britons stood out in strong relief. They were large of form, and strikingly beautiful. Taking an interest in them, Gregory asked from what country they were brought. He was told they were from Britain. He asked whether their people were pagan or Christian. "Alas!" he said, on being told, "that the author of darkness should be possessed of so fair subjects, and while so beautiful in outward aspect, their minds should be devoid of inward grace." "What was the name of that race to which they belonged?" On being informed that they were Angles, with some humour, he replied, "That is good, they have angel faces; and what is the name of the province from which they come?" It was Deira. "It is well," he said, "'de-ira'—withdrawn from the wrath of God, and called to the mercy of Christ." And what was the name of their king? He was told his name was Aella, and alluding to the resemblance of the name to Alleluia, he remarked, "It is fitting that the Name of God should be sung in those regions."

A few years after this he became Bishop of Rome. The incident had made a strong impression on him. He did not forget the British, and he sent his prior Augustine on a mission to Britain with a letter to Ethereus, Bishop of Lyons. Forty monks accompanied Augustine, and they reached England in the year 597, and landed at Kent. Ethelbert, the King there, had married a Christian princess, Bertha, who had her own Christian Bishop as chaplain. After a time the King was converted, and together with his chief

men and people of Kent, was baptized.[13] Then Augustine found himself confronted with the fact that there was a Church with Bishops already existing in Britain. He sought, through the mediation of Ethelbert, King of Kent, a conference with them, with a view to union in their missionary work. We may here notice that after the breaking up of the Roman colony in Britain, the inhabitants of Wales had grouped themselves into independent kingdoms, in each of which a separate bishopric had been established. The conference took place at what came to be called "Augustine's Oak," at the junction of the two present dioceses of Worcester and Hereford. We get a narrative of the proceedings from the historian Bede.[14] Augustine began by brotherly admonitions to preserve Catholic unity and unite in the blessed work of preaching the Gospel. He stated the differences between themselves and the Roman Church. It does not appear that there was any essential diversity in doctrine. The principal divergencies were in the time of keeping Easter, and some peculiarity in the mode of administering bap-

---

[13] Cutts' *Augustine of Canterbury*, 57.
[14] Bede's *Ecc. His.*, ii. 2; *Early Eng. Ch. His.*, Ch. lll., Bright.

tism, and the form of the clerical tonsure, which in the one case was a circle, and in the other a half moon, and some ritualistic peculiarity in the Ordination Office. The British Church had a Liturgy, and a version of the Bible of its own, and on all the great questions of the Gospel held the Faith as set forth by the General Councils. The British Bishops were not disposed to give up their special customs. They were not obliged to do so by any canon or moral law.

They stated that they had followed the customs of their spiritual ancestors, received through Gaul from St. John the Apostle.

Though St. Augustine is said to have worked a miracle in support of his views, the British Bishops declined to accept it as conclusive evidence, and postponed their decision to a future conference. Augustine then resolved to reduce his demands to the one point of keeping Easter, and their uniting under him as their Archbishop. A second conference was held.[15] The Britons, before coming to it, are said to have consulted with a certain holy and discreet hermit, who said, "If Augustine is a

---

[15] *Early Eng. Ch. His.*, p. 82, Bright; Cutts' *Augus. Cant.*, p. 141; *Bede, Ecc. His.*, ii. 2.

ST. AUGUSTINE AND THE BRITISH BISHOPS.

man of God, follow him." "But how shall we know that?" replied they. "Our Lord saith," he replied, "take My yoke upon you, and learn of Me, for I am meek and lowly in heart. It is to be believed that he has taken upon himself the yoke of Christ, and that he offers the same to you. If he is stern and haughty, however, it appears that he is not of God, and we are not to regard his words."

The Bishops replied again, "How shall we learn even this?" "Do you contrive," he replied, "that he may arrive first with his company at the place where the Synod is to be held, and if at your approach, he shall rise up to meet you, hear him submissively, being assured that he is the servant of God. But if he shall despise you and not rise up when you approach, let him also be despised by you." The old hermit's conduct reminds us of that of blessed St. Philip Neri, who, when asked to investigate the case of a nun said to be possessed of miraculous powers, walked to the convent, and having well soiled his boots by walking in the muddy roads, at the presentation of the nun to himself, requested her to pull them off. Accustomed to be treated with the reverence due to her supernatural powers, she declined to do so. The saint, returning to Rome, reported to the Pope, "No special humility, no miracle." The Bishops in our case, approaching the place of meeting, saw St. Augustine seated under the shade of a great oak tree. The British party consisted of seven monks from the convent at Bangor, who were also Bishops, and other ancient men, representatives of the old British Church. "Alas," says Bishop Browne, "Augustine retained his seat like a sovereign receiving a humble deputation from his subjects." The question was decided. Augustine was willing, he said, that if they would keep Easter at the due time, and unite under him as their Bishop, all other things would be tolerated. The British Bishops in their sturdy independence said they would not do any of these things. The conference thus failed, "but we must observe," says Professor Cutts in his history,[16] "that Augustine did not demand submission to the Roman See as of *divine right,* or pass any sort of sentence of excommunication upon the Bishops for their refusal." The Augustinian mission was not a permanently successful one. It lingered on with various vicissitudes until the time of Honorius. He died in the

---

[16] *Augus. of Canterbury,* Cutts, p. 146.

THE AMERICAN CATHOLIC CHURCH.   103

year 653, and was the last survivor of Bishops who traced their orders to Augustine. In time, the Augustinian succession, never large, died completely out. We quote from Dr. Browne: "As the weary old Italian, Bishop Honorius, slowly dying at Canterbury, looked forth upon the field that had been entrusted to his predecessors, he saw it covered with Christian laborers but not of his own sending, the ministers of a Church, not his." [17]

It would be ungracious, even unchristian, not to acknowledge the debt of gratitude we Anglicans owe to the great-hearted Gregory in sending Augustine, or fail to acknowledge his work as one of the founders of the Christian Church in the English part of Britain. But we must not fail, on the other hand, in our gratitude to those early missionaries, Ninian, Columba, Aidan, Felix, and others, who wrought the conversion and reconversion of Britain. Here we may quote from Bishop Browne: "Of all the seven kingdoms, there was only one, named Kent, which owed its conversion to the mission of Augustine. Of twenty-six counties in Britain, there was only one of which it can be said that it owed its permanent conversion to

---

[17] *Conversion of Heptarchy*, Browne, p. 186.

the mission of Augustine. With few exceptions, England owed its final and permanent conversion to the labors of the Scotic Church."[18]

How Theodore Became Archbishop.

In the summer of 664 occurred the "Yellow Pest," one of those plagues which have ravaged Europe from time to time. At that time the affairs of the Church in Britain were in confusion. The kings of Northumbria and Kent consulted with other kings concerning the obtaining of an Archbishop for the vacant See of Canterbury. They selected Wighurd, a good man and a fit priest; but he died of the pestilence. There was a monk, in Eastern orders, named Theodore, a native of St. Paul's birthplace, Tarsus in Cilicia, who had lately come to Rome in the train of the Emperor Constans II. He was sixty-six years of age; a man of learning both in secular and divine literature, and of holiness of life. Hadrian, Abbot of a monastery near Naples, and African by nationality, to whom the position had been offered, had suggested Theodore, whom he well knew, for the position. Theodore proved to be a man of great

---

[18] Browne's *Conver. Hept.*, p. 178.

energy and orthodoxy and sound judgment. It is to him that we owe the uniting of the various English churches into one province, over which he ruled as Metropolitan for sixteen years.

It was a great day, May 27, A. D. 669, when the "grand old man," as Dean Hook calls him, took his seat on the throne of Canterbury. On September 24th, A. D. 673, at Hertford, we find him holding the first provincial council. The old British Church had, in obedience to Apostolic rule or canon, kept up its synods, even when driven into the Welsh borders. Now the old and the new were united. This Council of Hertford, called by Theodore, was the first united synod. At it, Theodore first asked each of its members whether he agreed to keep the ancient and canonical decrees of the Fathers. This shows that the English Church did not consider herself independent of the common consent. She might legislate for herself, but her legislation must be in conformity with the whole Catholic Church. Theodore proposed ten canons based on the ancient law, all but one of which were adopted. This Council was indeed a most memorable one. It was the first of all the English national assemblies. It gave expression to ecclesiastical unity. It laid the foundation of our Church's solidarity. We may well regard Theodore, and those who coöperated with him, with loving gratitude.

The Danish Invasion.

We cannot give our readers a narrative of the English Church without mentioning a second invasion, this time by the heathen Danes, or Vikings. There had sprung up a nation of fierce, powerful warriors from the northern country around the Baltic Sea. They had gone up the great river-roads of Germany and France. They had become a terror to civilization. They had made settlements also in Ireland. They desired the subjugation of England in order to connect and consolidate their growing empire. They hated with an inexpressible hatred the Britons because they were Christians. The story of their various invasions is a long one. Their first recorded appearance was off the coast of France in 787. Six years later they destroyed the holy monastery of Lindisfarne. For a period of some seventy years there were constant raids on the English coast. And wherever they went, they burned the churches, destroyed monasteries, sacked them of their treasures, and massacred priests and women and children. In 866 they deliberately planned and carried out a scheme for the subjugation of the whole country. There were many instances of heroic courage and loyalty to the cause of Christ.

The Danes, under Ivar, invaded East Anglia. Their superiority in discipline, their reckless daring, and their skilful leadership, enabled them entirely to defeat the East Anglian forces. Ivar ordered Edmund, their king, to be brought before him. He demanded him "to divide with him his treasures, to reign as his lieutenant, and to abandon Christianity for the gods of the north."[10] "Who are you," so runs the haughty traditional message of Ivar, "that you should dare to withstand our power? The storm of the ocean is no bar to our enterprise, but positively serves us instead of oars. The roarings of the sky, its lightning flashes, have never injured us. Submit then to a master whom even the elements serve." "Tell Ivar," answered Edmund to the messenger bidding him abjure Christianity, "that I am not terrified by his threats. You may destroy this frail body;

---

[10] *Ch. of Eng.*, Dean Spence, p. 362.

death is more desirable than the service of demons." The savage Danish chief then took the king, bound him to a tree, scourged him with remorseless severity, then riddled the tortured body with arrows, and cut off his head. Another saint was crowned in heaven.

The Danes now turned their attention to Wessex. They sailed up the Thames in large force. The Wessex Christians made a sturdy resistance. Very many battles took place with varying success. And here we give another Christian incident. Early in the day of the battle of Ashdown, Alfred, then a young man, was left in command. Being hard pressed, he sent a messenger to his brother the king to send him reinforcements without delay. King Ethelred was hearing Mass, and engaged in the solemn prayer which he deemed the best preparation for the stern battle which lay before him. He bade the messenger of Alfred tell his brother that the king would come when the Mass was done. "God first, man after," were Ethelred's traditional words. In this case, the Christians conquered, but the Vikings received aid from the Continent. They were fierce, powerful, and skilful warriors. They pressed on their work

of subjugation, until Wessex was devastated and exhausted in resources, almost crushed out of existence. Then it was that King Alfred retired to a little secluded place in the marshes in Somerset called Athelney. Here for three months he waited, prayed, and gradually gathered about him a new force. Suddenly with great skill he surprised the Danes, who supposed the war was over, and defeated them. They fell back into the shelter of their armed camp, which Alfred besieged and took. The power of the Danes was broken. The peace of Wedmore was then concluded. The Danes by it were forced to leave England, or, remaining, to accept Christianity.

After the Danish Invasion.

The Danes, though conquered by Alfred, retained dominion in the northern part. Though the churches had been destroyed, and Christianity almost exterminated, a little band of Christians kept alive the faith at York. Gradually it extended, and the scattered Christians were brought together and some converts were made among the Danes, though the northern part was not recovered to Christianity till after the Norman Conquest.

In the south, however, Alfred bestowed much attention upon the revival of education. It was greatly necessary for the clergy, who had sunk into much ignorance. Alfred's policy was carried on subsequently by Edgar. He was greatly helped by the great Archbishop Dunstan. Dunstan was a man of brilliant talents, strong of will, of great devotion, and noted for his learning. A statesman, no less than an ecclesiastic, of striking personality, he infused a new life into the Church. He was at one time Abbot of Glastonbury, and made it a great centre for scholarship. He believed that the cause of education was the cause of religion. He was not only a great organizer, but a wise and practical teacher. Perhaps no years of his life were more fruitful than those when he was Abbot of Glastonbury. Subsequently he became Archbishop of Canterbury, where he ruled for seventeen years. Dunstan was the king's great counsellor. There is a story of St. Dunstan reproving King Edwy. At the coronation feast the king absented himself, preferring to be in the company of Elgiva, his betrothed, or bride. The nobles felt keenly the indignity of the king's leaving them, and sent Dunstan to bring him back.

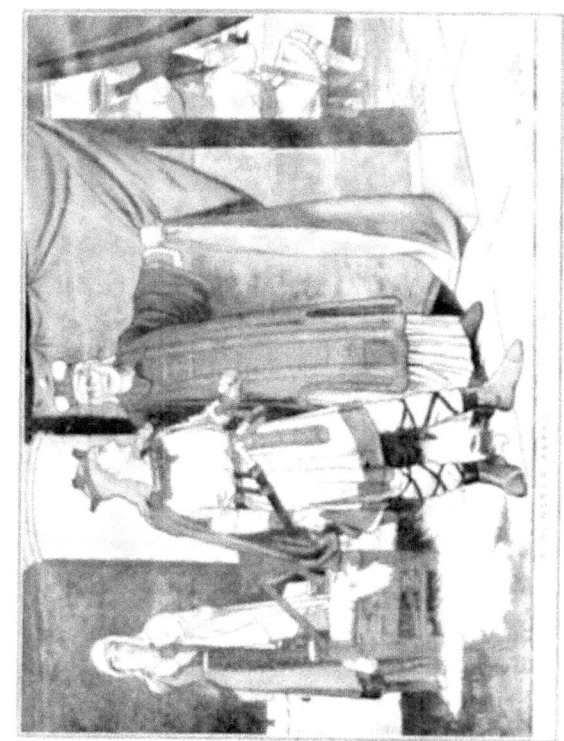

ST. DUNSTAN REPROVING KING EDWY.

It was not a pleasant duty to perform, but Dunstan succeeded, although bringing upon himself the undying hatred of the king, who, instead of regarding him for doing his duty, forced him into exile. He was the first of those great ecclesiastical statesmen who played such a prominent part in the history of England. He greatly encouraged the development of the monasteries, for he regarded the monastic system as necessary for the renewal of the Church's life. To their influence we greatly owe the recovery of the Christianity of England. At the time of his death, he was living a life of devotional retirement. He had a happy and peaceful ending to his career. On Ascension Day, 988, he preached three times in his Cathedral, and, it is said, with unwonted fervor and eloquence. On the Sunday following, he preached to the brethren, and summoning them to him, received the Body and Blood of Christ, and began the recitation of a psalm, "The merciful and gracious Lord hath so done His marvellous works that they ought to be had in remembrance. He hath given meat unto them that fear Him;" and with these words, he fell asleep.[20]

---

[20] Bede's *Ecc. His.*, Book IV. 5.

We here conclude our account of the Conversion of the Heptarchy.

We now, returning to the spiritual condition of the Church, state what had been the doctrine and worship during this long period.

Worship and Doctrine.

The Church was known in Britain as the "Church of England," and its worship and ceremonial bear witness to the continuity of the Church from the earliest times. As it had inherited the ancient faith, so it preserved the ancient worship. We have evidence of this from the canons of Edgar (959-975). They were made, it is stated by Cutts, under the influence of Archbishop Dunstan, and set forth a standard of life and morals for the clergy. They declare the great duty of the clergy to be to "celebrate the worship of Almighty God, to intercede for all Christian folk, to be faithful and obedient to their Bishop, and to be ready to help God-ward, and man-ward." "That all things belonging to the Church be worthily appointed, that there be always lights in Church at Mass; that there be no negligence about anything consecrated: holy water, incense, bread, or anything holy; that at the right time the bell be rung, and the priest say his Hours in Church, and that he resort there to pray, and to intercede for all. That no priest come into the Church or stall without his upper garment, or minister without his vestment. That every priest hear confessions, and give penance, and carry the Eucharist to the sick, and anoint him if he desires it; that every priest have oil for baptism and for anointing the sick. Let him promote Christianity in every way, as well by preaching as by good example, and he shall be rewarded by God." [21]

By these canons of Edgar's the priests were required to preach every Sunday, and to expound the Scripture. They were to teach people to pay their dues to God. They were to distribute people's alms so as to please God, and dispose people to almsgiving. They were to avoid drunkenness, and warn the people against it. They were to eschew unbecoming occupations, and to behave discreetly and worthily. The priest was not to be a hunter or hawker, but to occupy himself with his books, as became his order. He was to bring the books and vestments that they might be inspected.

[21] *Parish Priests in Middle Ages,* Cutts, p. 66.

He was to see that the children be brought within thirty-seven days to baptism. The priest was to forbid all well-worship, necromancy, or things which pertain to heathenism. The priests were to keep the Churches for the divine ministry and pure worship, and for nothing else. They were not to allow idle talking, ill deeds, unbecoming drinkings, nor any other idle practices in the vicinity of the Church. They were to take care that no one was buried in the church, unless he were known to be well-pleasing to God. The priest was not to celebrate the Eucharist in any house, only in Church, except in cases of extreme illness. He was not to consecrate, except on a consecrated altar. For this purpose, he had a proper slab of stone, which he used on journeys and in visitation of the sick. He was not to celebrate without a book and the canons of the Mass before his eyes, that he might make no mistake. He was to have a corporal when he celebrated, and all necessary things were to be rightly appointed. He must reserve the Host ready for any that had need. He must celebrate with pure wine and pure water. He must not celebrate Mass without partaking himself. Every one should receive fasting, except in case of extreme sickness. The chalice must be of molten material, never of wood. Such was the ceremonial of the Church of England, all in general conformity with the ceremonial handed down from Apostolic times.

The orthodoxy of the united Church, the "Ecclesia Anglicana," is seen in the utterances of the Council of Hatfield, 680, and the canons there formulated. The Synod declared its "acceptance of the true and orthodox faith as our Lord Jesus in the Flesh delivered the same to His disciples, and as it is delivered in the Creed of the holy Fathers, and of all holy and universal synods in general, and by the consent of all approved doctors of the Catholic Church." [22]

The Church then, as it does now, appealed to the whole Church for guidance. It is this principle that should govern our legislators.

We may observe for the benefit of some of our lay readers that there had been at the time of which we have been writing five holy and universally accepted councils. The first one, that of Nicea in 325, had been called together by the Roman Emperor, and was presided over by Bishop Hosius of

---

[22] *Docs. of Eng. Ch. His.*, Gee & Hardy, p. 13.

Spain. At Nicea, it was declared that our Lord was "consubstantial" with the Father. He was very God of very God. The second Council was called the First of Constantinople. It assembled in 381, and was presided over by Meletius of Antioch, Gregory Nazianzen, and Timothy of Alexandria. It proclaimed the deity of the Holy Ghost. The third in order was held at Ephesus, over which Cyril was president. It declared that there was but one Person in the Incarnate Lord. At Chalcedon in 451, the Council proclaimed the two natures, the Divine and the Human, in Christ. It was at this Council that Constantinople was erected into a patriarchate second to Rome. It held that the precedency of Rome rested on the political ground of its being the capital of the empire, and as the seat of the imperial court had been moved to Constantinople, it declared that it should be second in dignity. The Council thus ignored any claim of the Romans based on connection with St. Peter. The Fifth General Council met in 553 at Constantinople. It stated the truth that there were two wills in Christ. He was thus, by the General Councils everywhere accepted, "declared of one substance with the Father, God of God, possessed of two natures, with two wills, and the natures united in one Person." Subsequently the Sixth General Council was held, and the Faith there declared was recognized by the English Church by Synod held at Chelsea, 787. It was here that the Archbishops, Bishops, and Abbots vowed with all the devotion of their minds that "they would keep the decrees there promulgated to the utmost of their powers by the help of the Holy Spirit; that the Holy, inviolate Faith of the Nicene Council be firmly held by all, and that the priests of every Church profess, hold, and teach the Apostolic and Catholic Faith of the Six Councils, as approved by the Holy Ghost." [23]

It is to be observed that these Councils were not in the nature of a Supreme Court, or court of last resort. The Bishops did not come together to prove doctrines out of the Scriptures, or from other sources, but each to bear his independent witness as to what had been the Faith from the beginning. The unanimity of their testimony was a proof of its divine origin. And our Anglican Church to-day appeals as she always has appealed to the undisputed Councils and to the consent of undivided

---

[23] *Docs. Eng. Ch. Hist.*, Sec. viii. p. 32.

Christendom. She appeals for her test of doctrine to the common consent. She holds now to the old St. Vincent de Lerins rule, "*Quod semper, quod ubique, quod ab omnibus.*" In this age, when men are tossing about on the waves of unbelief and asking for some safe guide, the position of the Anglican Church cannot be too well understood. What this ancient Church of ours held, we, as Catholic Churchmen, hold to-day. As Lord Chancellor Selborne said, the doctrines and practices which the Church of England rejected at the Reformation were of mediæval, not of Apostolic, times, and they were unknown when the Church of England was founded, and for ages afterwards. He says: "If the authorized doctrine and practice of the Church of England at the present time should be compared with that of the Christian Church generally, including the Church of Rome, in the days of Augustine, it would require a strong application of the theological microscope to discover any real, substantial difference between them." [24]

---

[24] *Defence Ch. Eng.*, Selborne, p. 7.

BOOKS REFERRED TO IN CHAPTER IV.

Ecclesiastical History. Bede.
Documents of the Church of England. Gee and Hardy.
Augustine of Canterbury. Cutts.
Liturgy of the Celtic Church. Warren.
Early English Church History. Bright.

Much use has been made in this chapter of *The Conversion of the Heptarchy*, by the Rt. Rev. Bishop Browne of Bristol.

CHAPTER V.

THE DIVISION, EAST AND WEST.

A GREAT and terrible calamity happened in the Church of Christ. After a thousand years, in which a practical unity existed, Eastern and Western Christendom separated. Satan, who by the discipline of the Church was bound for a thousand years, now so far prevailed as to rend the Church asunder. This, which is one of the most important facts in Church History, is often overlooked or ignored, both by Roman Catholics and American Church laymen. "A knowledge of the claims of the Eastern Church," said Dean Stanley, "keeps up the equipoise of Christendom." If we wish to have a true view of Church history and Christian doctrine, we must not overlook the Eastern Orthodox Churches. We can as little understand the Church without taking the fact of the separation of the East and West into account, as we can understand

TROITZA MONASTERY, KREMLIN.

American history apart from the Declaration of Independence and our separation from Great Britain.

Long before the Anglican Reformation, with its rejection of the papacy, a like rejection had taken place; and a division had been created which has lasted to this day. This is a most important fact. It was on July 16, 1054, that the legates from Rome placed a document of excommunication on the high altar of the Cathedral Church of St. Sophia in Constantinople, and shaking the dust off their feet, hurriedly and in anger left the building.[1] It was a few days later, that the Eastern Church, acting through its Patriarch, returned anathema by anathema, by solemnly excommunicating the Church of Rome.

The principal causes of division were the insertion by the Romans of the "Filioque" in the Creed, and the Papal claim by divine authority for supremacy in the Church. The contention of the Easterners was in behalf of the ancient original form of the Creed and for freedom from papal domination.

---

[1] *Mother of All Churches,* Cole, Chaps. iii. and iv.

To understand the Eastern position, we must recognize the fact that the Church had gradually conformed its organization to the lines of the empire. The Roman empire was divided into about one hundred and twenty provinces. In a chief town of these provinces the Church had established a Bishop having some jurisdiction over local Bishops. There was thus in each province a metropolitan. The provinces themselves were divided into four or five exarchs, which came to be called patriarchates. The Bishops, or Patriarchs, outranked the metropolitans, and also took rank or precedence among themselves. So it came to pass that the Bishops of Constantinople, because it was new Rome, and those of Antioch, Alexandria, and subsequently Jerusalem, together with the Roman Bishop in the West, held a certain preëminence of honor and dignity above their brethren. The Bishop of Rome, however, had—by virtue of Rome's having been the capital, the wealth and generosity of the Church, its claim to be an Apostolic See founded by Peter and Paul, and by a growing assertion based on Peter's temporary leadership, and subsequently by aid of documents known as the Forged Decretals—assumed a position of lordship over the other Bishops. This assumed authority was not in the opinion of the Easterns supported by the testimony of Holy Scripture as interpreted by the Fathers. Nor was an absolute monarchical rule, according to their view, the true principle of unity, as declared by Christ. It was of human origin and man's love of power, and did not bear witness to the Church's divine mission. For this cause, and also on account of the independent Roman insertion of the "Filioque" into the original Nicene Creed, the great rupture between the East and the West took place.

The question of the Filioque, or the proceeding of the Holy Ghost from the Father *and* the *Son* was a profound theological question. There are two processions of the Holy Spirit, the temporal and the eternal one. No question is ever raised concerning the former. Our Lord after His Ascension sent the Holy Spirit to the Church. He said concerning the Holy Spirit, "I will send Him unto you." The question relates to the eternal procession, or the action which takes place in the divine Being Himself.

The Easterns, with their vigorous sense of the unity of God, declared, which is true, that there could be only one "source" or fountain of life in the Blessed Being of God. This is represented to us by the term "Father," who is the one source of Life in the Godhead. To hold, they said, that the Holy Spirit proceeded from the Father *and* the Son, would be in violation of the unity of the divine nature. It would in fact postulate two Gods. The answer made is that the Holy Spirit does not proceed from the Son in the same way that He proceeds from the Father. There can only be one source, it is true, in the divine life. The Holy Ghost, therefore, as the active principle of love, proceeds *from* the Father to the Son, who is the express Image of His Person, and in whom the Father delights, but proceeds back *through* the Son to the Father, as the manifestation of the Love of the Son to the Eternal Source. This statement concerning the Holy Spirit the Easterns are willing to acknowledge as theologically sound; but they further make objection that the term "filioque" was not part of the original Creed, and was put into it by the Western Church with the sanction of papal authority. For the East to admit this insertion would be for it to admit the whole claim of the papacy; a thing which it cannot rightly do.

THE AMERICAN CATHOLIC CHURCH. 125

If Christian fellowship and intercommunion between ourselves and the Eastern Churches is ever to be established, it will be necessary for us to add an explanatory note or to conform our recitation of the Nicene Creed to the original form.

There are to-day about eight millions of people under the Patriarchate of Constantinople.[2] The three ancient patriarchates of Alexandria, Antioch, and Jerusalem have now a comparatively small number of adherents. There are about three and a half millions belonging to the national churches of Servia, Montenegro, and Austro-Hungary, and four and a half millions to Roumania and Greece. There are about two millions or more under the government of what is called the Holy Synod. The Church in Russia is the largest in numbers and in influence. It is under the government of its Holy Synod, of which the Metropolitan of St. Petersburg is the presiding officer. Moscow was formerly a patriarchate, and it is not unlikely that this position will again be given it with the consent of the other Eastern Churches. There are about eighty millions of Russians in this Church, which

---

[2] *Papers and Reports of Eastern Ch. Assoc.; Synopsis of Oriental Christianity*, A. Riley.

has done a noble missionary work within its own borders and in the conversion of the northern part of Asia.⁸

It looks as though the Eastern Churches, regarded as a whole, though they have had to bear the brunt of the Mahometan conquest, have nevertheless, done a vast and glorious missionary work, and through divine charity have held together. On the other hand, if we look at the west, we find that the papacy has been a constant source of division, not a conservator of unity. For the Roman Church has lost the northern half of Europe, and is no longer a dominating influence with the Teutonic races, upon whom the future civilization of the world depends. It is also a decadent force among the Latin nations of France, Spain, Portugal, and even of Italy herself. While the papacy has become, by the decree of papal infallibility, more solid as a machine and man-made government, the decree has led to the revolt of some hundred thousand or more adherents, who have united under a valid Episcopate, with the title of "Old Catholics."

---

⁸ Smernoff's *Russian Orthodox Missions.*

In doctrine and worship, the Eastern Churches have been marked by their conservative spirit. They hold the doctrines declared by the Seven General Councils, and they take Holy Scripture as interpreted by the Fathers for their rule of faith. Like the Anglican Church, they reject the doctrine of the papal supremacy and Rome's modern declared doctrine of papal infallibility. Though having great reverence for the ever-blessed Virgin Mary, and devotion to her as the bringer-forth of the God-Man, Jesus Christ, they know nothing of the new Romish dogma of the immaculate conception of the Blessed Virgin Mary, nor do they hold, as Rome does, that the faithful departed hereafter suffer in the penal fires of a purgatory to satisfy the justice of God for forgiven sins.

They have their liturgy in a vernacular, which can be understood of the people. They give the Blessed Sacrament in both kinds. Their parish priests are married. They pray, as Christ prayed, and as the Church has ever prayed, for the departed. They believe in the Real Presence of Christ's Body and Blood in the Holy Eucharist. The Russian Church has, however, "dissociated itself from the Aristotelian teaching as to substance and accidents."[4] Their people practise confession to God in the presence of a priest, who, by absolution, assures them, being penitent, of their forgiveness. They ask of God, through Christ, a portion in the prayers of the saints, whom, as intercessors, they invoke. Their theory is that whom they may pray for, their prayers they may ask. Thus invoking the blessed Mother of God, they also pray for her. They believe in the communion of saints. Their doctrines are set forth fully in their catechism, which is far more comprehensive than ours, and based in all points on Holy Scripture. Their racial and oriental descent makes them more expressive in their devotions than ourselves. They often make the sign of the cross, and prostrate themselves in the Church's service. They stand praying before the sacred pictures or icons, but do not pray to them. Their catechism forbids this. It teaches them that when they look on them with their eyes, mentally to look to God with their hearts.

The Easterns show publicly an intense feeling of devotion and gratitude to God. After their de-

---

[4] *Mother of All Churches,* Cole, 54.

ST. SAVIOUR'S CHURCH, MOSCOW.

liverance from Napoleon, they erected the great and beautiful Church of S. Saviour, holding ten thousand people, at Moscow, to commemorate the event. The English, on the other hand, with their practical business spirit, built a bridge over the Thames, and called it Waterloo Bridge, as an outward expression of their victory.

As the Eastern Church is the inheritor of the earliest traditions, it is useful to study her forms of worship. The church building has a "naos," which, like our Anglican word "nave," signifies a ship. It declares the doctrine that the Church is the ark of safety. At the east end, there is a choir, or "soleas," which is a platform raised a few steps above the nave, where the choir, composed of men and boys, stands on either side. Here the deacon, leading the congregation, says the prayers and reads the Gospel. The soleas is separated from the sanctuary, or "bema," by a solid screen, called the "iconostasis." It has three doors, and is covered with sacred pictures or icons, which give the name to the screen. On either side of the central or royal door are icons representing our Lord and the Blessed Virgin. The iconostasis is made very beautiful and glorious with representations of the saints. Within the sanctuary or bema, stands, in front of the royal door, the Holy Table. The term Altar, we may observe, is given to the whole space within which the communion table stands. The latter is not long like those in the Western Church, but square. It is sometimes of stone, but oftener, we believe, of wood, as most like that of the Altar of the Cross on which Christ was offered. On it stands the book of the Gospels, elaborately bound and ornamented, and a pyx, containing the reserved Sacrament. A cross, which may be of silver, and is certain to be very handsome whatever the material, lies on the table. The two or more branch candlesticks which are used in the service are also to be found there. The Bishop's seat or throne, raised a few steps, is in the rear of the altar, with seats for the clergy on either side. On the north side of the sanctuary is a small chapel known as the "Prothesis."

Here the Holy Elements for the Communion are prepared. This is done most reverently and with a series of prayers. Here, too, the Priest vests for the service. Over the cassock he wears a "stoicharion," which corresponds to our alb, or long surplice. It is made, however, not of linen like

THE AMERICAN CATHOLIC CHURCH. 131

our own, but of silk or velvet. In addition, the deacon wears the "epimanikia," which are close fitting cuffs. These perhaps were originally adopted as a matter of practical use, like our amice, which serves as a collar to our alb. The deacon also wears the "orrarian," or stole. The priest wears both of these latter vestments, but the two parts of the stole are united so that it must be put on over the head through an opening in the top. At the Eucharist the priest wears the "phelonion," which corresponds to our chasuble. The Bishop wears an "epigonation," which hangs from his girdle to the right knee and is symbolical of the sword of the Spirit. The Bishop also wears a mitre, which, though unlike ours in shape, is much ornamented.

The Eastern Churches use the ancient liturgies of St. James and St. Chrysostom. It is pleasing to notice that there are portions of the service which we have in common with them. Like them, we have an office of Morning Prayer or Litany, which precedes the Eucharist. Our Epistle, Gospel, and Creed, and subsequent Consecration Prayer, proceed in the same order as theirs. Much like them, we have our glorious *Ter Sanctus*. The priest says, Lift up your hearts. *Chorus:* We lift them up unto the Lord. *Priest:* Let us give thanks to the Lord. *Chorus:* It is meet and right to worship Father, Son, and Holy Spirit, the consubstantial and undivided Trinity. *Chorus:* Holy, holy, holy, Lord of Sabaoth, heaven and earth are full of Thy glory; Hosanna in the highest; blessed is He that cometh in the Name of the Lord; hosanna in the highest.

Their prayers are much more full and devotional in expression than our classically condensed collects. They constantly speak of God as the good God, the Lover of mankind, and their canon or consecrating prayer has elements in it not unlike our own. Thus they pray, "O Lord, Lover of mankind, we cry and say, Holy and most Holy art Thou, and Thine only Begotten Son, and Thy Holy Spirit; Holy and most holy Thou, great is Thy glory; who so lovedst the world, that Thou didst give Thine only Begotten Son, that whosoever believeth in Him should not perish, but have everlasting life; Who came and fulfilled all things necessary for our salvation. Who in the same night in which He was delivered up, or rather did deliver up Himself for the life of the world, taking bread in His holy, spotless, and undefiled Hands, gave thanks, blessed, sanctified and brake it, and

THE KAZAN, ST. PETERSBURG.

gave it to His holy disciples and Apostles, saying, Take, eat; this is My Body, which is broken for you for the remission of sins." *Chorus:* "Amen."

"Likewise also after the Supper the Cup also, saying, Drink ye all of this, for this is My Blood of the New Testament, which is shed for you and for many for the remission of sins." *Chorus:* "Amen."

"Mindful, therefore, of this command of our Saviour, and of all things which He wrought for us, His Cross, His Burial, His Resurrection on the third day, His Ascension into Heaven, His Session on the right hand, His second coming to judge the world, in all and through all we offer unto Thee Thine own of Thine own." *Chorus:* "We praise Thee, we bless Thee, we give thanks to Thee, and pray Thee, Lord our God.

"Again we offer Thee this reasonable, this bloodless sacrifice and we beseech Thee and pray and entreat that Thou wouldst send Thy Holy Spirit upon us and upon these gifts lying before Thee.

"Bless, Master, the holy Bread.

"And make this bread the precious Body of Thy Christ.

"Amen.

"And this Cup, the Precious Blood of Thy Christ, changing them by Thy Holy Spirit, that they may be to those who partake of them for soberness of mind, for the remission of sins, for the communication of the Holy Ghost, for the fulfilment of Thy heavenly kingdom, for confidence in Thee and not for judgment. Moreover, we offer Thee this our reasonable service on behalf of those who are departed hence in the faith, our forefathers, fathers, patriarchs, prophets, apostles, preachers, evangelists, martyrs, confessors, chaste persons and for every righteous spirit perfected in the faith. Especially our most holy, undefiled, most blessed glorious lady, the bringer-forth of God the Ever-Virgin Mary. Amen."

The conformity of our own Liturgy with this most ancient one is obvious. It is noticeable that the Eastern Church not only asks the prayers of the Ever-Blessed Virgin, but prays for her. One of the most beautiful portions of their Liturgy is the great entrance when the elements are brought in, at what we would call the Offertory, when the Cherubic Hymn is sung:

"Let all mortal flesh keep silence; Let us that are mystically representing the Cherubim, and sing-

AN ICONOSTASIS.

ing to the life-giving Trinity the Tri-Sagial hymn, put away all the cares of this life: Since the King of all, invisibly escorted by the Angelic orders, we are about to receive. Alleluia, Alleluia, Alleluia."

This might on special occasions be fittingly introduced, with its music, into our service as an offertory anthem.

The Liturgy of the Eastern Churches is the most dignified, solemn, and devotional of any; and it is offered on every Sunday and holy day. Unlike the Roman Church, the Eastern Churches have no abbreviated service or Low Mass; and in fulfilment, as they believe, of the teaching in Malachi, "that in every place incense shall be offered unto My name, and a pure offering," they never celebrate without incense. They regard the abbreviated Western low celebration, with its absence of incense, as slovenly, undignified, and Romish.

As an independent witness of the ancient faith and worship and true Gospel teaching, their agreement with us, both as against Protestant negations and papal additions, is most valuable.

Their Doctrine.

In the reply made from Constantinople to the

late papal encyclical inviting them to union, the Patriarch, with his Bishops, said that the union of the separated Churches in one rule of faith is a sacred and inward desire of the Holy Catholic Orthodox and Apostolic Church. Their weighty words are worth considering. They said:

"The Eastern Church is willing to accept heartily all that the Eastern and Western Churches unanimously professed before the ninth century. If the Westerns prove from the Holy Fathers and the divinely assembled ecumenical councils that the Roman Church ever before the ninth century read into the Creed the addition of the filioque, or accepted the doctrine of purgatorial fires, or sprinkling in baptism instead of immersion, or the Immaculate Conception of the Ever Virgin, or the temporal power, or the infallibility of the Bishop of Rome, we have no more to say. But if, on the contrary, it is plainly demonstrated that the Eastern and Orthodox Catholic Church of Christ holds fast the anciently transmitted doctrines which at that time were professed in common both by the East and West, and that the Western Church perverted them by divers innovations, then it is clear that the way to union is by the return of the Western Church to the ancient doctrinal and administrative condition of things."

The Eastern Church, therefore, holds, in accordance with the words of Holy Scripture, that the Holy Ghost proceeds from the Father, and not also from the Son, as has been arbitrarily promulgated by the Western Church. She asserts that the ancient practice of baptism was by way of three immersions; that the divine Eucharist was celebrated for more than a thousand years with leavened bread; that following the divine command, "Drink ye all of it," the Holy Catholic Church had ever given the holy chalice to the laity; that the Apostolic Church, walking according to the divinely inspired interpretation of Holy Scripture and the Apostolic tradition, prayed and invoked the mercy of God for those who had fallen asleep in the Lord, but the papal Church from the twelfth century downward has invented a multitude of innovations concerning purgatorial fires, and a treasury of merits derived from superabundance of virtues of the saints, and the distribution of them by the Pope to those who need them.

The only holy Catholic and Apostolic Church of the seven ecumenical councils teaches that the supernatural Incarnation of the only-begotten Son and Word of God, of the Holy Ghost and the Virgin Mary, is *alone* pure and immaculate; but the papal Church scarcely forty years ago again made an innovation by laying down a novel dogma concerning the immaculate conception of the Mother of God and ever-Virgin Mary, which was unknown to the ancient Church, and strongly opposed at different times, even by the more distinguished among the papal theologians.

The Pope in his encyclical, represents the question of the primacy of the Roman Pontiff as the principal and, so to speak, only cause of the dissension, and sends us to the sources, that we may make diligent search as to what our forefathers believed, and what the first age of Christianity delivered to us. Having recourse to the Fathers and ecumenical councils of the Church of the first nine centuries, we are fully persuaded that the Bishop of Rome was *never considered as the supreme authority and infallible head of the Church*, and that every Bishop is head and president of his own particular Church, subject only to the synodical ordinances and decisions of the Church universal as being alone infallible, the Bishop of Rome being in no wise excepted from this rule, as Church history shows.

Moreover, the papists themselves know well that the very passage of the Gospel to which the pontiff of Rome refers, "Thou art Peter, and upon this rock I will build My Church," is, in the first centuries of the Church, interpreted quite differently, in a spirit of orthodoxy, both by tradition and by all the divine and sacred Fathers without exception; the fundamental and unshaken rock upon which the Lord has built His own Church, against which the gates of Hell shall not prevail, being understood of Peter's true confession concerning the Lord, that "He is Christ, the Son of the living God." Upon this confession and faith the saving preaching of the gospel by all the apostles and their successors rests unshaken. Such, then, being the divinely inspired teaching of the Apostles respecting the foundation and Prince of the Church of God, of course the sacred Fathers, who held firmly to the Apostolic traditions, could not have or conceive any idea of an absolute primacy of the Apostle Peter and the Bishops of

Rome; nor could they give any other interpretation, totally unknown to the Church, to that passage of the Gospel, but that which was true and right.

The divine Fathers, honouring the Bishop of Rome only as the Bishop of the capital city of the empire, gave him the honourary prerogative of presidency, considering him simply as the Bishop first in order, that is, among equals; which prerogative they also assigned afterwards to the Bishop of Constantinople, when that city became the capital of the Roman empire, as the twenty-eighth canon of the fourth ecumenical council at Chalcedon bears witness, saying, among other things, as follows:

"We do also determine and decree the same things respecting the prerogatives of the most holy Church of the said Constantinople, which is New Rome. For the Fathers have rightly given the prerogative to the throne of the elder Rome, because that was the imperial city. And the hundred and fifty most religious Bishops, moved by the same consideration, assigned an equal prerogative to the most holy throne of New Rome."

From this canon it is very evident that the Bishop of Rome is equal in honour to the Bishop of the Church of Constantinople and to those of other Churches, and there is no hint given in any canon or by any of the Fathers that the Bishop of Rome alone has ever been prince of the universal Church, and the infallible judge of the Bishops of the other independent and self-governing Churches, or the successor of the Apostle Peter and vicar of Jesus Christ on earth.

Each particular self-governing Church, both in the East and West, was totally independent and self-administered in the times of the seven ecumenical councils. And just as the Bishops of the self-governing Churches of the East, so also those of Africa, Spain, Gaul, Germany, and Britain, managed the affairs of their own churches, each by their local synods, the Bishop of Rome having no right to interfere, and he himself also was equally subject and obedient to the decrees of synods. On important questions which needed the sanction of the universal Church, an appeal was made to an ecumenical council, which alone was and is the supreme tribunal in the universal Church. Such was the ancient constitution of the Church.

"During the nine centuries of the Ecumenical Councils the Eastern Orthodox Church never recognized the excessive claims of primacy on the part of the Bishops of Rome, nor consequently did she ever submit herself to them, as Church history plainly bears witness."

"The Orthodox Eastern and Catholic Church of Christ, with the exception of the Son and Word of God, who was ineffably made man, knows no one that was infallible upon earth. Even the Apostle Peter himself, whose successor the Pope thinks himself to be, thrice denied the Lord, and was twice rebuked by the Apostle Paul as not walking uprightly according to the truth of the Gospel. Afterwards the Pope Liberius, in the fourth century, subscribed an Arian confession; and likewise Zosimus, in the fifth century, approved an heretical confession, denying original sin. Vigilius, in the sixth century, was condemned for wrong opinions by the fifth council; and Honorius, having fallen into the Monothelite heresy, was condemned in the seventh century by the sixth Ecumenical Council as a heretic, and the Popes who succeeded him acknowledged and accepted his condemnation.

"In vain, therefore, does the Bishop of Rome send us to the sources that we may seek diligently for what our forefathers believed, and what the first period of Christianity delivered to us. In these sources we, the Orthodox, find the old and divinely transmitted doctrines, to which we carefully hold fast at the present time, and nowhere do we find the innovations which later time brought forth in the West, and which the papal Church, having adopted, retains till this very day. The Orthodox Eastern Church then justly glories in Christ, as being the Church of the seven Ecumenical Councils and the first nine centuries of Christianity, and therefore the one holy, Catholic, and Apostolic Church of Christ, the pillar and ground of the truth; but the present Roman Church is the Church of innovations, of the falsification of the writings of the Church Fathers, and of the decrees of the holy councils, for which she has reasonably and justly been disowned, and is still disowned."

The above letter was signed by the Patriarch

of Constantinople, along with his comprovincials. There are thus eight points of difference between the Holy Orthodox and Apostolic Church of the East, and Rome. With four of these, we Anglicans are at one with the East. We give the Blessed Sacrament in both kinds, condemning Rome's denying the Cup to the laity. We deny the doctrine of a purgatory of penal fire, where the faithful must suffer to satisfy the divine justice, and from which they can be relieved by purchased or gained indulgences.

We agree with the East in refusing to accept the Roman doctrine of the immaculate conception of the Blessed Virgin Mary. We reject the Roman doctrine of papal infallibility, and the Pope's claim to be the absolute monarchical head of the whole Church Militant, endowed with all executive, legislative, and judicial powers. On two points the Anglican Church takes a middle ground: she allows the use of both leavened and unleavened bread; and she provides for immersion in baptism, but allows not sprinkling, but "pouring." The American Church distinctly invokes the Holy Ghost upon the Elements.

The real difference between Anglican and

Eastern Churches lies in the use of the "Filioque" clause, which we inherited from Rome. The recitation, as it was not in the original Creed, we might, for the sake of intercommunion, explain or omit. It would not hinder our future union with Rome, if that should be ever desirable, for, united to the East, Rome would accept us, as she has the uniat Churches, wherein the omission has been allowed. It would be a great aid to the cause of Christianity if, by the recognition of each other's Catholicity, intercommunion might be brought about between the Anglican and Eastern-Orthodox Churches. It is a happy sign that Bishop Raphael, head of the Orthodox Syrian Church in the United States, has given permission to his own people, where no priest of their own is present, to be baptized, and the marriage service performed, by an Anglican priest, and the Holy Communion received, under certain circumstances, at his hands. Kozlowski, the late Old Catholic Bishop, announced his willingness to take part in the consecration of an American Bishop of our Church. Prelates of both Churches have exchanged courtesies, recognizing each other's orders. But before any official action can be taken, there must be a more general desire on our part, officially expressed. Very different is the attitude of the Church of Rome from that of the Eastern Churches towards us. Rome imperiously demands an absolute submission to her papal claims and modern doctrines. This is on our part an impossibility, as it would be disloyalty to Christ. The East asks only if we hold the same faith. Can we not, ought we not, to lay aside our inherited prepossessions, and respond to the cry for union which comes from the heart of our Lord?

We Anglicans ought all to seek and pray for a united Christendom, for its divisions so greatly hinder the work of the Spirit in the conversion of the world. Two conditions are necessary before it can be accomplished. Our sectarian brethren must get a fuller grasp of the Incarnation, and recover their lost sense of the need of the Priesthood.[5] Their ministers are preachers, who disclaim the idea of their being priests. It cannot then be called illiberal in us to deny to them that which they repudiate for themselves. But priesthood is an essential element in Christianity. When sectarian clergy discover their loss, they will be desirous of

---

[5] See Ch. 1, p. 5.

Episcopal ordination. The other condition is that which relates to Rome. The Roman Bishops must seek for and recover their full Episcopal powers, now taken away by the Pope. When they have recovered them, the papacy falls, and the way to reunion is opened. If mutual recognition is ever brought about, it will be through Anglicans, the Old Catholics, and the Eastern Churches. Therefore the fraternal spirit of the latter should be lovingly responded to. While Rome demands an absolute submission to its monarchical claims and modern doctrines, the East only asks, "Do we hold the same ancient faith?—if so, we are brethren."

BOOKS REFERRED TO IN CHAPTER V.

Mother of All Churches. J. G. Cole.
Eastern Church Association Papers.
L'eglise Latine et le Protestantisme. Khomiakoff.
Teaching of the Russian Church. Headlam.
Greek Manual of Doctrine. H. T. F. Duckworth.
Russian Orthodox Missions. E. Smirnoff.
Catechism of the Orthodox Church. Tikhon.
Doctrine of the Russian Church. R. W. Blackmore.
Anglican and Eastern Doctrine. Rev. C. F. Hale.
Comper's *Handbook of Liturgies.*
Liturgy of St. Chrysostom and St. Basil. Robertson.
Service Book of Greco-Russian Church. Hapgood.
Answer of the Great Church of Constantinople to the Papal Encyclical.
Student's History of the Greek Church. A. H. Hore.

CHAPTER VI.

THE RISE AND DEVELOPMENT OF THE PAPACY.

THE MODERN claims of the papacy are something tremendous. Christ, it is said, "founded a visible Church, neither as an aristocracy, nor as a federation, but as an absolute monarchy." We quote from an accredited Roman Catholic authority.[1] The head of the Church, or the Pope, possesses the plentitude of power, including all legislative, judicial, and coercive authority; as supreme pontiff, he is able to make universal law, and to bind the universal Church by himself alone. He is not subject to any, even a General Council. All judicial power rests with him. From his judgment there can be no appeal. He is also possessed of coercive power. The pontiff's

---

[1] Humphrey, S. J., *Urbs et Orbis*.

power in this respect is independent of every other on earth. He has, moreover, supreme liturgical power. He can alter the liturgy at his pleasure, or add to it new devotions. His Episcopal power makes him bishop of the whole world. He has the sole right of appointing Bishops, and of removing them at his will. The jurisdiction of any Bishop may be validly withdrawn by him, without any showing of adequate cause or giving of any valid reason. He is, in other words, the absolute monarch of the Church; and all authority of all kinds is in him. This position he claims as of divine right, as given by Christ to Peter; and through St. Peter's Episcopate at Rome, he claims, it became the endowment of Peter's successor.

The modern papal teaching respecting the papacy is that our Lord first became visibly present on earth by His Incarnation. Secondly, by His invisible Presence in the Holy Eucharist, wherein He is silent but effective. Thirdly, in the person of the Pope at the Vatican, where He is vocal. "The Sovereign Pontiff," says Faber, "is the third Visible Presence of Jesus Christ among us."[2]

---

[2] Faber, *Notes*, etc., Vol. I., p. 338.

In an official document printed by license of Pope Gregory XIII., we find the following, the interpretation being given by a Jesuit father: "To deny that our *Lord God* the Pope has power to decree as he has decreed, would be deemed heretical."[3] Again it is stated concerning the Pope, "whom we regard as God, and whom we ought to listen to as though we heard God speaking."[4] "All the Pope's acts must be considered as God's acts." "The Pope can do all things God can do."[5] At the Lateran Council, 1512, the Pope was said to be "a second God upon earth."[6] After this, we think our readers will be inclined to quote II. Thess. ii. 4.

The Scriptural warrant for these tremendous prerogatives is very slender. The three texts cited in support of it are first, that of St. John xxi. 15 and 17, where our Lord bade St. Peter "shepherd the sheep and feed the lambs." The obvious meaning here is that St. Peter, as representative of the Old Dispensation, and the leader among the Apostles, was to lead the sheep belonging to the old

---

[3] *Guardian*, Dec. 30, 1910, p. 1843.
[4] *Mussus Episc. Bit. Comment*, c. 14, fol. 606.
[5] Decius, *Comment in jus pontifio*, Lec. II.
[6] *The Reformation*, Whitney, p. 21.

Jewish order and the Gentile lambs into the Christian fold. This is what he did. At Pentecost he brought in the Jewish converts, and, subsequently, in the ministration to the Roman Centurion Cornelius, the lambs, or first fruits of the Gentiles. But the command of the Lord gave him no authority over other shepherds.

It was clearly not only not given, but actually forbidden; for when St. Peter said respecting St. John, "But what shall this man do?" our Lord said, "What is that to thee?" or in plain English, "That is not your business." The second text that the Romans rest on is that of St. Luke xxii. "I have prayed for thee that thy faith fail not." We must believe that our Lord's prayer was answered; and the way in which it was answered shows what He prayed for. He did not pray that St. Peter should be possessed of any infallible gift, or that he should not deny the faith, for he did so. When Peter said, "I know not the *man*," He denied what he had previously confessed, *i.e.*, that Jesus Christ was the Son of *God*. What our Lord prayed for was that, though he should deny the Faith, nevertheless he might not lose his faith in Christ, and fall away from Him. Our Lord prayed that Peter should hold on to his faith in Christ. He did this, and repenting, and being forgiven, he was able to strengthen the faith of his brethren who had not fallen away as deeply as he had. "The application of this text to the papal claims is," says Professor Robertson,[7] "a very late after-thought. I know," he says, "of no such use of it earlier than the year 681."

Again, let us take the third text which Romans cite in support of the claims of the Papacy. Our Lord did not say, "Thou art Peter, the *Rock* on which I will build My Church." But on this Rock, this very Rock, I will build it. Now the word "Rock" as used in the Old Testament signifies God. It is reserved to the Almighty. Thus it is written, "Who is a Rock, save our God?" "God only is my Rock." "Is there a God beside Me? Yea, there is no Rock, I know not any." "Their rock," *i.e.,* the heathen's god, "is not as our Rock." Thus to the mind of the Apostles, the term Rock would refer to God.[8] Therefore when Peter had confessed Christ to be the Son of *God,* and our Lord had said, "On *this Rock* I will build

---

[7] Robertson's *Roman Claims,* Ch. His. Soc., xiii.
[8] Wordsworth, *Com.,* S. Matt. xvi.

My Church," the Apostles would naturally understand Christ as referring to Himself.

Most of the Fathers, when explicitly interpreting this text, say that the Rock is Christ, or the confession of His divinity. Some few refer it to Peter, but none see in it a gift or office bestowed on him, which he was to transmit to a successor. Launoii, a learned Roman Catholic writer, analyzing the statements of seventy Fathers, cites forty-four signifying that the Church was founded on the Apostles; sixteen said the Rock was Christ; seventeen that it meant Peter, but none of the latter assigned to Peter an office which was to be passed on to another.[9] The true position of St. Peter is brought out fully in the book, *Christian and Catholic*, by the author of this work. It may be sufficient here to quote the words written by the late learned Roman Catholic Archbishop of St. Louis, Dr. Kenrick, who in a speech which was to have been delivered before the Vatican Council said that the text in St. Matthew, as interpreted by the Fathers, did not bear out the Roman contention. "If we are bound," he said, "to follow the majority of the Fathers in this

---

[9] Launoii. Vol. X., 103, 106.

thing, then we are bound to hold for certain that by the 'Rock' should be understood *the Faith professed by St. Peter, not Peter professing the Faith.*"

Again: the Apostles must have understood Christ's words correctly, seeing they received "the Holy Ghost to lead them into all truth." Now there is one sure test to show in what way the Apostles understood Christ's words. There is no evidence in Holy Scripture that the Apostles understood Christ's words as giving to St. Peter any authority or jurisdiction over themselves. The Lord expressly forbade any such exercise of authority of one over the others, and said, "It shall not be so among you." He placed all the Apostles on an equality, as sitting alike on twelve thrones; each was to be like the other, one of the twelve foundations. Cardinal Newman said "of the first twelve Apostles not one was possessed of universal jurisdiction." Christ was the chief cornerstone, in whom the whole building was to be joined in unity. The twelve, all alike, were the foundations united to, or laid on, Him. Christ was also, as He declared, "the Vine"; and the Apostles, including Peter, were only branches. Peter was first, the leader of the original twelve, the foundation layer of the Church, the bringer in of the Jews and Gentiles, but the idea of any supremacy of St. Peter over the other Apostles finds no foundation in Holy Scripture.

Nor is there any explicit mention in the New Testament that St. Peter was ever at Rome; or that as Bishop of Rome he conveyed any special privilege to a successor. Now the right to convey to another a "privilege" must be explicitly stated in the original grant, and its conveyance proved by explicit testimony. Peter's right to convey to another his special office finds no warrant in Holy Scripture, nor his doing so any proof in history. The lack of sure testimony in Scripture makes it clear that no doctrinal importance can be connected with Peter's being at Rome. It is impossible to think that God would have made our salvation dependent upon our being under the jurisdiction of Rome, and not have certified us in Holy Scripture of the fact of Peter's holding the Episcopal office there. Every historical fact on which Christianity is based and found in the Creed is recorded in Holy Scripture. If St. Peter's being at Rome is one of these essential matters, it should in like manner be found there, otherwise it is obviously to be held not essential, and no doctrine can be based upon it.

Again: not only does Holy Scripture not place Peter over the other Apostles, but there are many texts in the New Testament, in the Acts and the Epistles, that show that all the Apostles were of equal authority. Bartoli, who after many years of service in the Jesuit order has lately left the Church of Rome, cites some forty texts to this effect.[10] A full list can also be found in Brinckman's *Notes on Papal Claims*. "The New Testament does not give us," says Professor Robertson, "the slightest hint that the Apostolic Church bequeathed the Papacy to the succeeding age, not a hint that the words, 'Thou art Peter,' fixed the Constitution of the Church of Christ as a monarchy under a visible Head."[11]

Development of the Papacy.

How then can we account for the rise and development of the papal power? Some Roman disputants or apologists have contended that, though the papacy cannot be proved from Holy Scripture,

---
[10] *Prim. Ch.*, G. Bartoli, 66-67.
[11] *Rom. Claims to Supremacy*, Robertson, p. 210.

nevertheless it is the tradition of the Church. This argument, however, breaks down in face of the fact that such is not the tradition of the whole Church. It is only the tradition in that portion of Christendom that is under the jurisdiction of the papacy. The argument thus falls into the fallacy of a logical circle, viz., Rome is right, because she says she is right. The modern Roman defence again has sought to account for it on the theory of development. The most clever defender, or perhaps author, of that explanation was Cardinal Newman. We may grant that there was a progressive order in the development of the papacy. But the order of progress does not declare the *legitimacy* of the progress. We all may grant that the papacy has come about by development, but the question remains whether it was a development under the inspiration and guidance of the Holy Spirit, or whether it had a worldly motive as its determining principle. While we may admit that God can overrule the wrong-doings of men to His own purposes, yet that does not condone the wickedness of their actions nor put a seal of approval upon them. Now the development of the papacy has come about through the evil principle in man of the love of power. Just as has been told us, the love of money is the root of all evil, the love of power is the most disastrous of all the evil influences that affect man. It was the sin in Satan that led to the fall of the angels. It has been the ruin of kings and statesmen. It existed in the Apostolic College itself. The Apostles disputed among themselves "who should be the greatest." This spirit thus early manifested brought forth the severe rebukes and warning of our Lord.

It was not, however, exterminated. It led Rome first to a spirit of boasting and self-assertion. Very different, we may see, is the tone of St. Clement, of the sub-apostolic age, in his letter to the Church at Corinth, and that of Pope Victor (189-199), writing to the Bishops of Asia. Clement does not even mention himself. He makes no attempt on his part to speak as the successor of St. Peter; but Victor's threat to excommunicate all those who did not agree with him about the time of keeping Easter is in the spirit of self-assertive arrogance. That was the beginning of the bad power-loving spirit. It rightly brought forth from St. Irenæus the characterization of the Pope's conduct as "petulant intolerance."

It was also condemned subsequently by Pope Gregory the Great, who said: "No one of my predecessors ever consented to use so profane a term as 'Universal Bishop,' because, plainly, if a simple patriarch is called 'universal,' the name of patriarch is taken from the rest. Wherefore let your Holiness in your letters never call any one 'universal,' lest, in offering undue honour to another, you should deprive yourself of that which is your due. Whoever calls himself, or desires to be called, an 'universal' priest, in his pride goes before Anti-Christ."

It was the position of the Imperial City as the capital of the Empire, the wealth of the Church of Rome, the munificence of its gifts, its being the first Apostolic See in the West and the first in rank among the five patriarchates, that gave it its original preëminence. The love of power led on to the falsification of testimony on its behalf. This is to be seen in the misquotations made by Romanists. How often was St. Augustine quoted as saying, "Rome has spoken, the case is finished." He did not say this. Two separate clauses are put together, as if they were one. This is cited as if St. Augustine laid it down as a general principle.

He was confining his remarks to a particular case. "The misquotation," wrote Drs. Bright and Liddon, "is one of the most scandalous in all literature." Sometimes Roman arguers cite the saying of the Archbishop of Milan, "Where Peter is, there is the Church." Ambrose is thinking of St. Peter's confession of the faith, and of this confession of the faith being the foundation of the Church, and he speaks of Peter as taking the "first place in confession, not in office; in faith, not in order." A passage from St. Irenæus is often misquoted as saying: "With this Church, *i.e.*, Rome, because of its superior preëminence, every Church that is faithful everywhere, must agree." But he does not say "must agree." His meaning is that as Christians from all quarters of the world assemble at the Capital City, there the universal tradition has been preserved.[12] "One cannot," says Dr. Bright, "pass by two specimens of fiction contained in the Roman Breviary. On April 26th, Roman clergy are still bound to recite the lying legend of the Council of Siunessa, and its declaration that the first See could be judged by no one,

---

[12] Puller, *Primitive Saints*, 31, 43. Bright, *Roman See*, 29, 36. Salmon, *Infallibility*, 375. Simpson, *Papal Infallibility*, 11-14.

THE AMERICAN CATHOLIC CHURCH.   161

and on January 16th there is an extract from the monstrous forgery of the Forged Decretals, telling how Pope Marcellus "proved to the Churches of the Province of Antioch the primacy and the headship of the Church of Rome." We might go on with many other like instances. In a book published in 1875, and dedicated by special permission to Pius IX., we find the author, Vincenzi, saying that the Peter withstood by St. Paul was not St. Peter the Apostle, but some other Christian of that name.[13]

This spirit of falsification is also to be seen in the well known case of its quoting the canons of the provincial council of Sardica to the African Bishops in the case of Appiarius, as if they were canons of the ecumenical council of Nice.[14] On reference to the original copies preserved in the East, the Church of Alexandria proved the falsity of the Roman claim, and forbade appeals to Rome from its decisions.

Again: we find Rome backing up its spiritual prerogatives by the utterances of the Forged Decretals, of which *Janus,* written by two former

---
[12] *Notes on Papal Claims,* Brinckman, p. 182.
[14] *Rise of Papal Power,* Hussey, p. 49.

Roman Catholic professors, says: "It is difficult to find in all history so huge and successful a forgery."[15] These decretals were eagerly seized upon by Pope Nicholas I. in support of the new claims put forward by himself. In the contest with the East, the Pope then in power asserted that these decretals had ever been retained in the Roman archives. This was either an unintentional mistake, or else a falsification. As the Pope could have discovered these documents if they existed, it looks like wilful error. The decretals, though now acknowledged by Rome to be forgeries, entered into the canon law of the Church, and formed the basis on which the modern claims of the papacy rest. The claim that the Emperor Constantine made a gift of a portion of Italy to the Roman Pontiff, which has been often quoted to uphold the temporal power of the papacy, has likewise been proved a forgery. Well may we ask, with a Roman Catholic professor, Gratry, "Does God need man's lies to forward or uphold His Kingdom?" As time went on, the papal thirst for power showed itself in the claims of Hildebrand (1073-1085) and Innocent III. (1198-

---

[15] *Pope and Council,* Janus, 99-150.

THE AMERICAN CATHOLIC CHURCH. 163

1216). The Popes then claimed to be the overlords of all earthly rulers, and to have the right to absolve their subjects from all allegiance to their sovereigns when they did not obey the papal behests. Thus Boniface VIII. in 1300 appeared at Rome dressed in imperial habit, with two swords borne before him as emblems of his temporal as well as spiritual dominion over all on earth.[16]

The love of power leads on to persecution, and to the claim of the right to crush out heresy by force. Thus the Pope excommunicated kings, and laid their lands under interdict. Interdicts stopped all the ordinary exercise of religion. They deprived the people, to the risk of losing their souls, of the Gospel and Sacraments which Christ had ordained. It was the big club that the Pope held over kings and people.

This claim to depose sovereigns is still made by Rome. Cardinal Allan in 1882, in a book called *Letters to the Brompton Oratorians,* said, "No monarch so manifestly used his authority for the destruction, not the good, of the commonwealth as a heretical prince. No one, therefore, so justly deserves to lose his throne as he." "Men greeted

---

[16] Brinckman, *Notes on Papal Claims,* 213, 216.

as an act of supreme justice the solemn deposition of an heretical king." The righteousness of using force in suppression of heresy is still manifested. Pius IX. in his syllabus condemned the proposition that "the Church has no right to employ force." Leo XIII. wrote a letter of commendation to Professor Marianus on his work which strongly upholds the right and duty to coerce, flog, imprison, burn, and kill its opponents. Archbishop Manning in 1867, in *Essays on Religion and Literature,* wrote: "The right of deposing kings is inherent in the supreme sovereignty which the Popes as Vicegerents of Christ exercise over all Christian nations. When for the common good the Head of the Church exercises his supreme authority, either by excommunicating individuals, by laying nations under an interdict, *and by deposing kings,* all Christian people are bound to obey his decree." Lord Acton, a Roman Catholic and one of the most able scholars of the last century, said, "A man who thought it wrong to murder a Protestant king would be left for hell by half the Confessors on the Continent." [17]

Further, the love of power cannot but manifest

---

[17] *Letters to Miss Gladstone,* Lord Acton, p. 234.

itself in worldliness, luxury, and sensuality, qualities which have again and again been the characteristic marks of the papal See. It has led candidates for the papacy again and again to buy their way to the papal throne by bribes and simony. Again, when the Popes of Rome have been not morally rotten, they have been, in many instances, merely worldly-minded statesmen. The stories of so many of the early Popes having been martyrs are legendary fictions.

Again, the element of deceit has marked the papacy. It has been stated that all the holy Fathers, from Hermas in the first century, without a single exception, thought the Pope to be infallible in the sense of the Vatican Decree of 1870! This statement is a monstrous falsification. Professor Zimmer says, "The spirit of deliberate falsification in the interests of the Church only appears in the Irish Church after her union with Rome." [18]

Persecutions.

We come to the rise of the Inquisition. It was held by the Church of Rome to be right to torture and burn heretics. The tortures and sufferings

---
[18] *The Celtic Church,* p. 117.

inflicted thus are too painful to record.[19] The numbers may be exaggerated, but in 1482 two thousand persons are said to have been burned at Seville.[20] The terrible horrors of Smithfield have never been forgotten by the English people. It is true there were persecutions in the reign of Queen Elizabeth, but there were comparatively few victims. During the short reign of Mary, three hundred persons were put to death. There is, moreover, this to be said: Protestantism has again and again denounced the practice and repented of it; while among Romans to this day there are those who uphold it. In this respect Rome has not changed. And what shall we say of the massacre on St. Bartholomew's Day? To crush out what Rome believed to be heresy, she justified this awful crime. The Pope had a medal struck off to commemorate that wholesale slaughter.

Rome's Deceitfulness.

To-day, the deceit of the Pope's being a prisoner at the Vatican is imposed on the ignorant in the United States for the purpose of obtaining donations for his support. The Italian govern-

---

[19] *Letters to His Holiness*, by a Modernist, 25-42.
[20] *Letters to His Holiness*, by a Modernist, 34.

THE AMERICAN CATHOLIC CHURCH. 167

ment offered to place some $650,000 at his disposal yearly. He refused this on the ground that he had been deposed from his temporal sovereignty. Yet it was his Italian Roman subjects who deposed him.

The decree of a personal infallibility has consolidated the papal monarchical authority. May we not ask whether this papal development, brought about by the greed of power, is the work of God, or has God's approval upon it?

Has God Blessed the Papacy?

Contrast the two Churches, the Eastern and the Roman. While the Eastern Churches have done a magnificent missionary work in Russia and Northern Asia; in the West, the Pope has lost the northern half of Europe and England.[21] Instead of being a source of unity, it became, in the West, a cause of further division. The Hildebrandian policy in the papacy met an awful punishment from God. For seventy years, from 1309-1379, the seat of the papacy was at Avignon in France. During this time the Popes were elected under the supervision of the French king; they main-

---

[21] *Missions, Russian Church.*

168   THE LINEAGE OF

tained their court by his permission; followed meekly the policy he dictated. Corruption, sensuality, and luxury abounded. No sooner was the Captivity, as it has been called, over in 1377, than the great Schism ensued. For about forty years the Roman Church was torn asunder, and nine Popes in turn formally excommunicated one another. Different nationalities took different sides, and it was impossible for the faithful to know who the true Pope was.

Changeableness of Doctrine.

We are forced by Rome's assertion that she alone is the Church to examine her claim to be the one sure and safe guide in the Christian faith. It is not to be denied that, though claiming unchangeableness in doctrine, she has changed, and that she is now found to be asserting that to be essential which, formerly, she declared not to be so. In the last century, her Bishops in Ireland formally declared to the British Government, in order to obtain political privileges, that the infallibility of the Pope was not an article of their creed. In the Keenan Catechism, put forth in the last century with Roman authority, the question is asked,

"Must not Catholics believe the Pope in himself to be infallible?" The answer given is, "This is a Protestant invention, and is no article of the Catholic Faith." In a book of thirty-five selections, entitled *Roman Catholic Principles,* it is stated, "It is no matter of faith to believe that the Pope is in himself infallible, separated from the Church, even in expounding the Faith." In the Middle Ages, according to the decrees of the Councils of Pisa and Constance, a general Council was held to be superior to the Pope, and many appeals were made from papal decrees to general Councils. Now it is declared that the Pope is by himself superior to a general Council, and no appeal lies from him to one. In respect of the Immaculate Conception of the Blessed Virgin, Archbishop Kenrick wrote: "The Church never delivered it as a doctrine of faith, and Popes have strictly forbidden that the opposite opinions should be branded with the mark of heresy."

Attitude Towards Science.

And what are we to say concerning Rome's relation to science, and scientific discovery? It is an historical fact that the Pope and his inquisition condemned Galileo for holding that the sun relatively stood still, and that the earth had a diurnal revolution."[22] It has been argued in reply that the papacy may err on matters of fact, but not in doctrine. But the decision of the court in this case was not merely that Galileo's doctrine was scientifically untrue, but that it contradicted Scripture and was theologically false. After a full and careful examination of the case, Professor Salmon thus concludes: "Is it possible for the Church of Rome to err in her interpretation of Scripture, or to mistake in what she teaches to be an essential part of the Christian faith? She *can* err, for she *has* erred. She has made many errors more dangerous to men's souls, but never committed any blunder more calculated to throw contempt on her pretensions in the minds of all thinking men, than when she persisted for about two hundred years in teaching that it was the doctrine of the Bible, and therefore an essential part of the Catholic faith, that the earth stands still, and that the sun and planets revolve daily round it."

---

[22] Salmon, *Infallibility*, 230-253.

Purgatory and Indulgences.

Rome's doctrine of purgatory is also novel and without patristic authority, and is repulsive to the Christian conscience. It is not in agreement with that of the Orthodox Eastern Catholic Church. It declares that the faithful, though forgiven, must suffer hereafter to satisfy the divine justice. This does not seem to be in accord with the Lord's Parable of the Prodigal Son. God may, for remedial purposes, allow the consequences of forgiven sin to remain, or a punishment to follow as a warning to others, when the sins have been of a public character, like that of David. But has not Christ made a full satisfaction to God's justice, and is He not the only One that can do so? Here, however, we shall only state the nature of this punishment which, according to Rome, awaits the believing and penitent Christian. The Abbé Louvet, in 1880, wrote a systematic treatise on purgatory. He thus described it: "At the centre of the earth is the place of the damned; above it lies purgatory, divided into three regions. Above purgatory is the limbus infantium, inhabited by unbaptized infants, above that is the limbus patrum, now empty, formerly dwelt in by the souls liberated on our Lord's descent into Hades. We learn that the lowest division of the three mentioned is largely tenanted by the souls of priests and Bishops and monks. The Bishops, with mitres of fire on their heads, and a burning cross in their hands, are clad in chasubles of flame. The average time of detention for a Christian of more than usual sanctity, one who has never committed a mortal sin, is a hundred and twenty-three years, three months, and fifteen days. These are not, moreover, years of mere earthly measurement, as witnessed by the revelations of the departed." Louvet proves this thus: There were two priests who were friends, to one of whom it was revealed that he would be released from purgatory at the first mass that was offered for him. His friend on his passing flew to the Altar and offered it. The departed soon appeared to him, and said, "O faithless friend, here I have been for years in the avenging flames, and neither you nor my brethren have had the charity to offer a single mass for me." There are many other revelations of like character which Louvet quotes from departed priests.[23]

---

[23] Salmon, *Infallibility*, 206-214.

In a work by Michael Muller,[24] we read: "From the smallest spark of this purgatorial fire, souls suffer more intense pains than all the fires of this world put together could produce. In the fire, they suffer more than all the pains of disasters and the most violent diseases. They suffer more than all the most cruel torments undergone by malefactors or invented by the most barbarous tyrants. They suffer more than all the torture of the martyrs summed up together. Our terrestrial fire was not created to torment man, but the fire in purgatory was created by God for no other purpose than to be an instrument of His justice." As relief is to be obtained by masses which are to be paid for, this doctrine has been, and is, a great source of pecuniary profit to Rome. She represents those departed crying out with heartrending voices, "Father, mother, have pity on me, your child." "Brother, have pity on me, your brother"; "Sister, have pity on me, your sister." "Husband, have pity on me, your wife": "Wife, have pity on me, your husband." Purgatory and Indulgences

---

[24] M. Muller, *Souls in Purgatory*, 35-46.

174   THE LINEAGE OF

are a great source of revenue to the Roman Church and are an oppression and hardship to the poor.

MARIOLATRY.

The position of Mary in the Roman system is different from that of the ancient Fathers, or, indeed, the Catholic Church. First, she is said by her gifts to be different from all other human beings. It is declared that, "in the first instant of her human existence, she had the full and perfect use of her intellectual faculties."[25] She never lived that she did not also think, and understand, and know, and purpose, and determine, and resolve, and will." She was thus different from us.

Again: she is not merely regarded as a saint, or the very highest of saints. She has an office and position in the mystical Body of Christ. She is called the "neck" of the Church,[26] as Christ is called its Head. As in the physical order the blood flows from the head through the neck into the body, so it is held or taught that all graces that come from Christ pass through Mary to us.[27] "No grace is dis-

---
[25] *Mary Magnifying God*, Humphreys.
[26] Faber, *Notes on Doctrinal Subjects*, Vol. I., 280.
[27] Faber, *Notes*, Vol. I., 312.

pensed to men without passing through the hands of Mary." Devotion to her is therefore held necessary to salvation. "Let us fly to thy feet, O sweet Queen, if we would be certain of salvation." "He fails and is lost who has not recourse to Mary."

Again: the modern doctrine represents Mary as the merciful one, while Jesus, the Head of the Church, is the representative of Justice. It is easier therefore to go to Mary, and obtain succour and help through her, than it is to go to Him, who said, "Come unto Me all ye that labor and are heavy laden, and I will give you rest." [28] Wearing her scapular (a piece of brown cloth, on which are pictures which represent Mary, and to which strings are attached, so that it may be tied about the shoulders), is held to be a means of deliverance from eternal flames. This is assured by her deliverance from the souls in purgatory, over whom she rules. Pope John XXII. declared that she appeared and informed him that she would descend into purgatory each Saturday and take out of the flames of torment those who wore the scapular when they were on earth. This belief was

---

[28] Pusey, *Rule of Faith*, 51-58.

also confirmed and made a matter of faith by Pope Alexander V., Clement VII., Pius V., and Gregory XIII. The tendency of such teaching is to substitute a mechanical means of salvation for a living faith. The apparition of the Blessed Virgin Mary at Lourdes is held to be proved by the cures that are wrought there. But these are no more proofs of doctrine than are the cures and wonders certified by the followers of Swedenborg, Edward Irving, the Mormons, Dowie, and Mrs. Eddy. We are warned in Holy Scripture about believing in such visions and signs.

The prayers offered to the Blessed Virgin are not merely the hyperbole, or exaggerated expressions of devotion, as some Romans have contended, but imply that she holds a position as the Saviour of sinners derogatory to the supreme position of Christ. It is said that "Mary so loved the world, that she gave her only begotten Son." It is held that all who are saved, are saved only through her means and advocacy. So far has this idea of the union with her been carried, as to imply that she is given to us along with Him in the Eucharist. What shall we say, indeed, to such paraphrases of the *Anima Christi* and the *Te Deum* as the following:

"Soul of the Virgin, illuminate me;[29]
Milk of the Virgin, feed me:
Passage of the Virgin, strengthen me:
Make me always to trust in thee;
From all evil protect me;
In the hour of my death assist me.
Prepare for me a safe way to thee;
That with the elect I may glorify thee
For ever and ever.
We praise thee, Maker of God.[30]

We acknowledge thee, Mary the Virgin:
All the earth doth worship thee:
Spouse of the Eternal Father
To thee all angels and archangels,
Thrones and principalities, faithfully do serve.
To thee the whole angelic creation
With incessant voice proclaim
Holy, holy, holy, Mary.

Commenting on Roman devotions to Mary, Dr. Pusey wrote: "Surely, we may ask with St. Athanasius, Whence or from whom did they learn this? Who of the Fathers taught it? How is it that none of the Apostles delivered this teaching to those after them, or for so many hundred years the Church knew nothing of it?"[31]

While Roman devotions to Mary have diminished worship to Christ, in no portion of the

---
[29] Cusack, *What Rome Teaches*, 136.
[30] Robertson, *R. C. Church in Italy*, 235.
[31] *Rule of Faith*, 51-58.

Church has the doctrine of the Incarnation and the adoration of the God-Man been better preserved than in the Anglican Communion.

Unity of the Church.

Christ prayed that His Church shall be one, even as He and the Father were one. Now, the unity in the Divine Life is a unity of Nature. This unity is an eternal and indestructible one. So it was to be in the Church. Its members were to be united to Christ in baptism, and by the Sacraments, and so to be made members of Him. They would form altogether, as it is said in the Scripture, "the family of Jesus Christ." As being born again by baptism, they would form one family or generation. Thus the union that binds its members together is to be like unto the union that binds the brothers and sisters of a family in one. The baptized are one, because they all partake of one nature, viz.: the nature of Christ. This is that unity for which Christ prayed; it is an indestructible unity, and will have an eternal duration. It will thus be like that organic unity which binds the Father and the Son together. As no amount of quarreling among the members of an earthly family can destroy the family unity which comes from the common descent, so no amount of quarreling in the Church can destroy its unity. Brothers and sisters may quarrel, may refuse to speak, or to acknowledge one another; but this cannot affect the unity of the family. They are still brothers and sisters, whatever they may say or do. Thus all the quarreling within the Church cannot destroy its unity. The gates of hell cannot prevail against it.

But "union" is a different thing from "unity." The family is one from its common descent. But its members can quarrel, and it may become a disunited family. This is what has taken place in the Christian Church. Our Lord prayed, however, not only for unity, but for *union* among His followers. He prayed that they might be so united together that the world might recognize the supernatural power and divine mission of His Church as sent by Him. Now it is this fellowship and communion which the Church has lost, to the great injury of its spiritual and missionary power. The principle of this union was to be found in the divine charity which makes men of one mind in a house. It was divine charity and humble submission to the authority of the universal Church which was to keep the local Churches united. Such love and humility would witness to the indwelling of the Holy Spirit and enable men to realize the supernatural mission of the Church. It is in contrast with this that Rome has set up, as a principle of union, submission to the monarchical power of the papacy. There is nothing supernatural in the papal conception, which is of the earth, earthy, nor has it wrought to the preservation of union.

It is mainly through this papal conception that the Church has become divided into East and West, Latin and Anglican, Rome's unscriptural and uncanonical claim to supremacy being the cause of the division. She is the creator of schism, is a schismatical Church, and is in schism everywhere.

Papal Fallacies.

"The Church, being a kingdom, must have a head." It has. Christ is the Head. It does not, however, follow from its being a kingdom that the part on earth should have a separate head.

Another point out of which Romans make much is that the Church on earth, being a visible society, must have a visible head. Our answer is, that visibility requires a visible organization, but not one visible head. So it must be with the Church. Every family or nation has a head, and so has every Diocese; but it does not follow from this fact that there should be a visible head over all Bishops, any more than that there should be one king over all nations. Pope Leo XIII. said that because Christ was about to withdraw His visible presence, it was necessary He should appoint some one in His place. To this we agree. He did so by sending the Holy Spirit as His invisible Vicar, and the Bishops collectively to be His visible representative. Again, Romans say in all governments there must be a supreme court of appeal, and the Pope occupies that place. But there is this difference: the Supreme Court often alters its opinions, when it finds out its mistakes, but an infallible Pope cannot deny what he has said, however erroneous it may be. The system breaks down not only because Popes have contradicted themselves, but because Romans differ as to when the Pope speaks infallibly.

Again: a third assertion, often heard from advocates of the papacy, is that the Anglican clergy have no authority for their teaching. This is not true. Their authority is that of the whole Catholic Church, what it has held from the beginning unanimously, and says now. Our authority is the Living Voice of the whole Church. Again, it is said the "papacy is the only source of union." As a matter of fact, it has been the great principle of division, and by demanding new doctrines as terms of communion, is the great creator of schism. Again, "there are divisions in doctrine and ritual in the Anglican Church." There have always been some divisions. High and Low Churchmen differ: one party emphasizes the objective, and the other the subjective, side of religion. But the differences between them are more in expression than in essentials. The Church's ritual is wisely comprehensive, and the Prayer Book, as the authorized voice of the Church, is a safe and clear guide to all humble souls.

Finally the Roman advocate says: "You admit that Romans can be saved; we do not admit that Anglicans, being outside the Church, can be saved." Certainly, we admit that good Romans can be saved, but we do not say that Anglicans who deny the Sacraments and leave their post are in a safe position.

The Development of the Papacy.

Let us now make a resumé of the development of the papacy. We may divide it into five periods. The first period embraces the first six centuries, down to the time of Pope Gregory I. The Bishop of Rome was then looked up to with filial regard, as the first of the Patriarchs, and often consulted as the head of the Apostolic See of Western Christendom. His responsive letters were termed "epistles," and not, as subsequently, "decretals." Undoubtedly his influence was great. The second period extends from Gregory I. to Clement VI. (1046). This was a period of the growth of papal claims, extension of patriarchal power, claims of supremacy that led to the division between East and West. The Pope begins to call himself in this period "Vicar of Christ." The third period was the age from 1046 to the end of the Crusades, and was the age of its greatness, when it reached its climax under Hildebrand and Innocent III. The fourth period was that marked by its decline. It covered the time from the removal to Avignon to that of the Reformation. The papacy became nationalized, and lost its former international position. The Great Schism, when there were conflicting Popes, lost for it spiritual power, while the worldliness and luxury of the Renaissance affected its moral standing. At the Reformation, it lost its hold on Northern Europe. The last period, or modern papacy, though no longer sunk in immorality, has become by its definition of papal infallibility a solid political machine. It is quite outspoken in its defiance of modern thought. It has lost the adherence of the intelligent classes in Southern Europe. It is chiefly strong in theory and assertion. The claims of the papacy, however, will not bear the test of Scripture, the Fathers, or history. It took centuries for the Germanic and Anglo-Saxon people to learn the falsity of the papal claims. Truth percolates slowly from sound scholarship to the masses, but at last it comes. When the intelligent Roman Catholic clergy and laity shake off the bondage of forbidden investigation, and examine the foundation of the papal claim, they will revolt from it. They will recognize the distinction between Catholicity and papacy, and see that Christians may be Catholics without being papists.

The Vatican Council.

Lastly, let us consider the Vatican Council of 1869. According to Dr. Döllinger, it violated the principles of the ancient Councils. The subject of the Pope's infallibility, though dealt with, was not put in the summons to the Council. What right had it then to deal with that subject? On arriving, the Bishops found that they were not in the exercise of the ordinary right of members to elect their own officers. The presidents and officers of the Council had been appointed by the Pope. Freedom to bring forward motions or propositions was denied. No proposition could be brought forward unless it was approved first by a committee nominated by the Pope. The great principle always governing councils, as Döllinger says, "that nothing should be done in matters of faith without practical unanimity," was ignored. Quite a number of Bishops left the Council, among them some of the most able and learned, who were not present at the final promulgation. The scene of this, as described at the time, was a portentous one.

Rarely, if ever, do we read, did such a storm of thunder and lightning break over the city. In the midst of the gloom and darkness, the Pope read, in the increasing dimness of the church, the declaration his henchmen had prepared. A singular mark of God's interference followed. The next day, the Franco-Prussian war broke out, and France was obliged to withdraw her troops, which had been the protection of the papacy, from Rome. The Italian troops, welcomed by all patriotic Italians, entered Rome, which became then the capital of the united kingdom of Italy. The temporal power of the papacy fell, never to be revived.

This then is our conclusion: the papacy is the development of an evil principle, and submission to it is no way to union. It is to be observed that we are not speaking against Catholicity, but the papacy, and while we attribute the development of the papacy to a worldly motive, we believe that God loves the Roman Communion and raises up many saintly souls in it. God's Holy Spirit has been, in the last century, calling the Anglican Church to reclaim its Catholic heritage, and the Church has been responding to Him. The same

Holy Spirit, it would seem, has been pleading with Rome to return to Catholicity, and she has, we grieve to think, rejecting Him, become less Catholic and more papal.

AN ANGLICAN'S DUTY.

It is to be observed that the practical question before our Church to-day is, not which party was more in the right, Rome or England, at the time of the Reformation, but who is in the right to-day? The teaching and claims of Rome are now far different from what they were then. Since the Reformation, Rome has denied our orders, and has added to the Faith two dogmas which were unknown as such in primitive times. She has added the Immaculate Conception of the Virgin Mary and the Infallibility of the Pope. She has consolidated in the Pope all power, executive, legislative, and judicial. We may well, as loyal Churchmen holding the ancient faith, shrink from accepting any such claims. We may well hold back from running the risk of sinning by denying our sacraments and deserting our post.

To any one tempted to this sin, let us say, moreover, that the issue between Rome on the one side, and the Eastern and Anglican Churches on the other, can rightly be decided only by a free General Council.

It would be gross self-assertion for an individual to assume such powers. Even if granted, for the sake of argument, that the Eastern and Anglican Churches were in the wrong, and that Rome, in its claims for supremacy, is in the right, nevertheless, since no Ecumenical Council has decided in favor of Rome, it cannot be the duty of any one to act on his own private judgment and join her. We could not be condemned at the Judgment Seat of God if we should not do so. On the contrary, if Rome is in the wrong, and the Eastern and Anglican Churches are in the right, to leave our Church, denying its Sacraments, and deserting one's post, is to commit a grievous sin against our Lord and the Holy Spirit, which will stain our whole life and destroy our claim for reward for any work we may do. And if any have fallen into this sin, the only way to make reparation is, however humbling it may be, to return to the old Mother Church.

BOOKS REFERRED TO IN CHAPTER VI.

History of the Popes. Bower & Ranke.
Milman's *Latin Christianity.*
Baronius' *History.*
Pope and Council. Janus.
Primitive Church and Primacy of Rome. Bartoli.
Papal Supremacy. Robertson.
Petrine Claims. Littledale.
Primitive Saints and the See of Rome. Puller.
Roman Claims to Supremacy. Robertson.
Rise of the Papal Power. Hussey.
Infallibility. Salmon.
Papal Infallibility. Sampson.
Life of Bishop Grosseteste.
Launoii's *Works.*
Hallam's *Middle Ages.*
Anglican Brief Against Roman Claims. Brinckman.
The Papacy During the Reformation. Bishop Creighton.
Church of England versus the Roman Church. Patterson.
Souls in Purgatory. Michael Müller.
Roman See and the Early Church. Bright.
Papal Claims. Seymour.
Maria Sanctissima. Keller.
Letters from Rome in Councils. Quirinus.
Romish Indulgences of To-day. Fulona.
The Privilege of Peter. Jenkins.
Roman Catholic Churches in Italy. Robertson.
The Reformation. Whitney.

CHAPTER VII.

THE CHURCH OF ENGLAND IN THE MIDDLE AGES.

IT IS POSSIBLE, in this short space, to state only a few historical points that mark the period from the Norman Conquest to the Reformation. We may divide them under the heads of the relation of *the Church to the Crown,* the relation of *both* to the *papacy,* and the *training and condition of the clergy.*

I. What was the relation of the Church to the Crown? On the establishment of the Norman rule, a change took place in the administration of justice. Whereas before, the Bishop had sat in the shire-mote, along with the sheriff, in the administration of the law, civil and ecclesiastical, matters were now separated, and ecclesiastical causes were determined by the Bishop, sitting alone in his own court. An appeal might be taken

from him to the Archbishop's court, and in certain cases to Rome. This division had its advantages, which were in favour of the Church.

But the division into civil and ecclesiastical cases was not well defined. The Church claimed jurisdiction, not only over her own criminous clergy, but over all cases *involving* crime, and finally in the matter of probate of wills. The division of Bishops' court from sheriffs' court had two results: it made the clergy a privileged class, and it led to a system of canon law, with the Pope as supreme judge. It could not but, in time, bring on a clash with common law, which recognized the king as the fountain of national justice. The contest came to a head in the issue of investitures. The newly-appointed Bishop had been accustomed in England to do homage to the King, and to receive from him the Episcopal ring and the pastoral staff, as symbols of his political authority. The Popes had begun to denounce this practice, and it had been condemned in a Roman Council. A fierce and bitter struggle took place in England between Archbishop Anselm and King Henry I.[1] It was at last settled by the King's abandoning his

---
[1] *Docs. of Eng. Ch. His.*, p. 64.

right to invest with ring and staff as symbols of spiritual authority, but retaining the oath of homage to himself on the bestowal of the temporalities, and the acknowledgment of feudal allegiance and obedience.

The contest between the Church and State came up later, in the case of King Henry II. and Archbishop Becket. The king was determined that clerical privileges should be made subservient to royal prerogatives. Becket stood for the rights of the clergy and the necessity of resisting the royal encroachments. In one matter, the king seems to have been in the right. There had been a separation of the secular and the ecclesiastical courts. All clerical offenses, whatever the cause, were to be tried in the latter. However great their crimes, the clergy were only liable to be punished by the ecclesiastical courts, and not, as lay criminals were, in the State criminal courts. Under the easy way in which the tonsure for Holy Orders was then given, there arose a body of unprincipled men who were protected by the law from the just punishment due their evil deeds. The king proposed that the cleric condemned in the ecclesiastical court should be remitted to the secular one for sentence. Becket refused to accept this innovation in the law.

In 1164, the king produced a certain declaration, which from the place of its issue came to be known as the Constitutions of Clarendon. It declared that no Bishop should leave the kingdom without the king's consent, nor should appeal be taken to Rome without his leave. Both of these were ancient customs of the realm. The Constitutions declared a new principle: that the higher clergy held their land by barony; and that, on a vacancy occurring, the rents and profits reverted to the Crown. Whatever might be the history of the thirteen clauses of the Constitutions of Clarendon, to Becket they seemed a tyrannous expression of an arbitrary and masterful will.[2] The story is a long one, how the quarrel between King and Prelate grew in intensity, till at last, in a moment of anger at Becket's excommunication of himself and his barons, the king broke out in words which were interpreted to mean a desire for the Archbishop's life. Four armed knights hastened to Canterbury and entered the Cathedral, crying out, "Where is

---
[2] *Docs. of Eng. Ch. His.*, p. 68.

the traitor?" "Here," said Becket, "is the Archbishop, no traitor, but a priest of God." His dignity and saintly presence for a moment awed them. But, fired with an unquenchable hatred, they struck him down, and his brains lay scattered on the pavement.[3] This savage deed roused all England. It turned the hearts of the people in Becket's favor. They forgot all else, and saw in him only one who had lost his life in defence of their rights as against a tyrannous king. The result was that the Constitutions of Clarendon became much of a dead letter. No further check was made to appeals to Rome. But the law remained that papal bulls could not be introduced into the country, and that none of the king's subjects could leave it without the king's consent. It was also allowed by the king that no cleric should be sentenced by the civil court. Thus, on the whole, the Church succeeded in her struggle with the Crown.

This condition led to many scandals, "when the papal courts," as Wakeman says, "became far more corrupt than the king's courts," and the national ecclesiastical law became worse administered than the king's criminal law. A state of affairs

---

[3] *His. Ch. Eng.*, Wakeman, p. 115.

MURDER OF ST. THOMAS A BECKET.

began to exist exactly contrary to that with which Becket had to deal. The relation between the two powers became ever in a state of conflict, and ever needing readjustment, and it has continued so to the present day.

II. What was the relation of the Church and the King at this period to the papacy?

The Norman Conquest brought England into closer relationship with the Continent and the Pope. The English Church, united under Archbishop Theodore, had regarded the Pope as the first Bishop in Christendom, with whom its Bishops were joined in Christian fellowship. The English Church had been peculiarly a national one, with practically no outside authority which it was bound to obey. The English selected their own Bishops. The Church made its own canons, which needed no other authority. The Norman Conquest brought about a change. The Pope had blessed the enterprise of William of Normandy in coming over to England, which was subdued in a few years. Before William's disciplined soldiers, armed with sword and bow, the English, with their more primitive weapons of axe and javelin, went to defeat. The Normans were Christians, but with a Roman training. Their Bishops and priests had been educated in the Roman theology. Therefore they brought a Roman element to England. A number of the old Bishops and clergy were removed, and Normans were placed in their Sees and parishes. Two Roman legates came over, and at the Synod of Winchester, Stigand, the old Archbishop, was deposed. This was the beginning of a series of important interventions in English affairs on the part of the papacy.

Then, in the eleventh century, after the papacy had sunk to the lowest depths of degradation, and three abandoned women had ruled at Rome,[1] there came a reaction. There arose an imperial and powerful Pope, Hildebrand, who claimed, as from God, authority over all kings and their people. He was the possessor of the two swords, of all temporal and spiritual power. Kings of the earth held and ruled as delegated by him and under him. He could remove them, and absolve their subjects from all obedience. He could excommunicate them, and lay their lands under interdict. He could thereby deprive all their subjects of all of the offices of religion. It was a fear-

---

[1] *Lat. Christianity,* Milman. Baronius.

THE AMERICAN CATHOLIC CHURCH. 197

fully tremendous claim and power. Hildebrand wrote demanding that William's subjects should pay him Peter's pence. He also demanded that the king should, in acknowledgment of his papal sovereignty, do homage to him for his crown. William replied that he would not hinder his subjects from giving freewill offerings to the Pope, but as for submission for his own crown, he said, "Fealty I have never willed to do, nor do I will to do it now. I never promised it, nor do I find that my predecessors promised it to yours." [5]

The same spirit of independence of Roman assumptions was shown by Rufus. There were rival Popes. Anselm, the Archbishop, honoured one, the king the other. The Archbishop fled to Rome, and the king would not reinstate him in his See. The Pope sent word that if the king would not reinstate Anselm, he would excommunicate him. The king's reply was that he would tear out the Pope's messenger's eyes if they should come to England. They did not come.

Another papal imposition was a money one. From the end of the twelfth century to the Reformation, the consistent aim of the papacy was to ex-

---

[5] *Docs. of Eng. His.*, p. 57.

tend its authority, and to use it for the purpose of obtaining money. The account given in Wakeman's late history is as follows: "In 1226, Pope Honorius III. demanded for himself the grant of two prebends in each Cathedral. In 1229, Gregory IX. claimed a tenth of all movables from both clergy and laity. Later, by his legate Otho, he assessed a fifth of all ecclesiastical revenues. In 1246, Pope Innocent IV. demanded a third of the revenues from all vacant incumbencies. In 1258, Alexander IV. excommunicated the clergy who had not paid their dues.

"Moreover, the Pope began to claim the right of appointing to English benefices. He not only appointed when there was a vacancy, but before the vacancy occurred. This practice was called the system of papal provisors. The Pope often used his power in nominating personal friends, Italians, and in selecting those who never went near their Sees, but only drew their revenues. He bade Bishop Grosseteste install his nephew, a mere boy, in a canonry, a thing which the Bishop refused to do. By this system, the revenues of the most valuable benefices passed to non-resident Italians. In 1231, Gregory IX. forbade the English

Bishops to appoint to any benefices until some friends of his had been provided for. In 1239, he tried to extend the system to benefices in private patrons' hands. In 1240, he required the Bishops of Lincoln and Salisbury to find benefices for no less than 399 foreigners. It was calculated by Bishop Grosseteste in 1253 that the revenues derived by foreign ecclesiastics from English benefices amounted to three times the royal revenue. In 1256, Alexander IV. laid claim to the first fruits, called annates, of the emoluments of bishoprics. The whole system is said to have brought into the papal exchequer no less than £160,000 in the forty years preceding the quarrel between Henry VIII. and the papacy."

The Church and State at different times passed laws against the whole system. There was the Statute of Provisors, passed in 1351, which made the obtaining of a benefice from the Pope in derogation of the rights of patrons an offence punishable by law. This was followed, in 1353 and in 1394, by the Statutes of Praemunire, which forbade appeals to foreign courts, namely, the Popes, under penalty of outlawry.[6] In the time of Car-

---
[6] *Docs. Eng. Ch. Hist.,* Gee & Hardy, p. 122.

dinal Beaufort it was declared that no legate should come unasked into the kingdom. It was this venality on the part of Rome, and its oppression, that roused the nation, especially the laity, and led the way to the Reformation.

No less severe was the contest between the Pope and the nation in the time of King John, who had basely surrendered his trust, and done homage to the Pope as receiving the kingdom from him. All know how the great Archbishop, Stephen Langton, and the Barons met at Runnymede, and signed the *Magna Charta.* That great Charter declared the *Ecclesia Anglicana* free to have its own laws and liberties. This declaration has been cited by Roman Catholics as showing how the Church was on the side of progress and liberty. But it has not always been remembered that the Pope stood by John and pronounced *Magna Charta* to be null and void. The papacy has not been on the side of the people, save on the few occasions when it has been its interest to be so.

III.—CONDITION OF THE CHURCH.

It is more agreeable to turn now to the consideration of the Church and clergy during the Mid-

ARCHBISHOP LANGTON PRODUCING BEFORE THE BARONS THE CHARTER OF HENRY I.

dle Ages. The Church developed under the Normans, who were Christians; and Churches began to be multiplied. There was also a considerable revival of the monastic spirit, and many noble monasteries were founded. Lands and money were freely given for their endowment. In Saxon times the land had been divided into parishes; now we find the establishment of Vicarages, which were served by monks from the neighboring monasteries. A striking social feature of the time was the way in which the Church gathered her ministry from all classes of the people. The lords of the manor might present their younger sons, and the vicars might be the nominees of the Religious houses. The middle classes, however, supplied a great number of the clergy. There were also cases where a serf obtained leave from his lord to send his son to school. There were always some who took a less liberal view; and we find, even in the vision of Piers Plowman, the more liberal sentiments satirized. He says that bondsmen and beggars' children belong to labor, and should serve lords' sons, and that lords' sons should serve God as belongeth to their degree. When this principle was urged at the Reformation at the founding of

King's School at Canterbury, Archbishop Cranmer resisted it, saying, "To exclude the poor man's son from benefits of learning, is as much as to say that Almighty God should not be at liberty to bestow His gifts according to His most goodly will and pleasure."

The career that mother Church thus threw open to all extended not only to the offices of the Church but also to those of the State. From the monastery or cathedral school, the earnest or ambitious student went to some more famous centre of learning, to Boulogne for law, to Paris for theology, to Salerno for medicine, in England to Oxford or Cambridge, which were organized universities early in the thirteenth century. The clergy were not, unless by their own will, uninstructed.[7] The course of reading was, in the grammar schools, four years in the Latin language, literature, rhetoric, and logic, three years in science, *i.e.,* arithmetic, music, geometry, and astronomy. Afterwards seven years' study in theology, and three years in the Bible. They went up to the university at about fourteen years of age. In the thir-

---
[7] Cutts' *Parish Priests,* p. 139.

teenth century there were about 3,000 students at Oxford.⁸

An interesting account of his own life is given by Bishop Latimer in a sermon preached before the king, which gives us an account of the farmer who sent his clever son to school.⁹ "My father," he said, "was a yeoman, and had no lands of his own, only a farm of three or four pounds a year by the uttermost, and hereupon he tilled as much as kept half a dozen men. He had a walk for a hundred sheep, and my mother milked thirty kine. He was able, and did find the king a harness and his horse. I remember that I buckled on his harness when he went to Blackheath Field. He sent me to a school, or else I had not been able to preach before the King's Majesty now. He kept hospitality for his poor neighbors, and some alms he gave to the poor, and all this he did of the same farm." ¹⁰

It was easy for the student to get into minor orders, but he could not be priested without passing the Bishop's examination, and obtaining a title, *i.e.*, a definitely assigned place where he

---
⁸ Cutts' *Parish Priests*, p. 140.
⁹ Cutts' *Parish Priests*, p. 140.
¹⁰ Cutts' *Parish Priests*, p. 140.

could practise the ministry. There were, of course, a number of men whose vocation became wrecked, as is the case now. We find the worldly and unconverted clergy throwing off the clerical habit and adopting the secular dress of the time. From disciplinary canons which were made, we learn of their wearing girded belts, rings on their fingers, and long beards, and concealing their tonsure. We see, in our own day, clergy asserting that they are "men before they are priests," throwing off the clerical attire and wearing a secular dress. "Clergy then persisted," says Cutts, "in wearing their hair cut like other people's, and short skirted coats, and their ordinary dress was of red or blue, or other colors, instead of grey or black, and they ofttimes carried a short sword."

The costume worn in Church continued to be practically the same as in early times, a long under-garment or tunic, white, with long sleeves, known as the alb. At the time of Augustine, the chasuble or plenida, had come into use, and continued to be worn during the Middle Ages. The arearium, or stole, was placed round the neck, and was enriched with an embroidered border, the deacon wearing it over one shoulder. The amice was a square piece of linen which was put over the head before the chasuble was put on, and served to protect it from being soiled. The dalmatic was another over-garment, and shaped like a short tunic split at the sides, which became the distinctive vestment of the deacon at mass. A little later than the tenth century, the sub-deacon wore a tunical, which was a similar, but somewhat scantier, vestment. The cope was simply a cloak. It was originally a protection from the weather. It appears as a clerical vestment about the end of the ninth century, being worn in processions and in choir. The surplice, a shortened alb, which is the most modern of all vestments, came to be used in the saying of the divine office. In the Cathedrals, the Canons wore over the surplice a short furred coat or cope.[11]

The priests were bidden to address the people on the Lord's Day in sermons. Bishop Grosseteste, 1235-1254, gave directions to his clergy to preach on Sundays, and gave them the heads of their teaching. Bishop Exeter drew up a similar book for his clergy, requiring every parish to have a copy. Bishop Breitingham of Exeter assumed, in

---

[11] Cutts' *Parish Priests,* 191-195.

his directions, that a sermon was preached in all parish churches on Sunday. Other Bishops put forth similar injunctions. The subjects given them to preach upon by the Provincial Synod of Lambeth in 1281 were the Fourteen Articles of Faith, the Ten Commandments, the Two Evangelical Precepts of Charity, the Seven Works of Mercy, the Seven Deadly Sins, and the Seven Sacraments of Grace. Five of these Sacraments, it was declared, ought to be received by every Christian: Baptism, Confirmation, Penance, Holy Eucharist, and Extreme Unction. The two other Sacraments of Order and Matrimony were for individual application. The prayer to be said by the sick before receiving unction, is declarative of the evangelical spirit found in the Church. "My God, my God, my mercy and my refuge, Thee I desire, to Thee I flee, to Thee I hasten to come. Despise me not, placed in this tremendous crisis, be merciful to me in these my great necessities. I cannot redeem myself by my own works, but do Thou, my God, redeem me, and have mercy on me. I trust not in my merits, but I confide rather in Thy mercies, and I trust more in Thy mercies than I distrust my evil deeds, my faults, my great faults. Now I come to Thee because Thou failest none, I desire to depart and to be with Thee. Into Thy hands, O Lord, I commend my spirit; Thou hast redeemed me, O Lord God of truth. Amen. And grant to me, my God, that I may sleep and rest in peace, who in perfect Trinity livest and reignest God, world without end. Amen." [12]

The priests had many homiletic books to help them in their delivery of sermons. Among them were the *Speculum Christiana,* by John Wotton, Parr's *Oculii Sacerdotis,* put out in the year 1350, and *Libra Festivalis,* by John Myrk. There were also works of a spiritual character such as *The Prick of Conscience,* by Richard the Hermit, 1349, and the *Speculum,* by Archbishop Rich. The people were provided with various books of private devotions. There were primers, and layfolk's mass books, which explained the meaning of the service and the ritual. *The Mirror of Our Ladye,* was a popular book with the devout laity.[13]

Worship of the Church.

There were daily services in the Churches. Amongst the higher classes were to be found do-

---
[12] Cutts' *Parish Priests,* 126-240.
[13] Cutts' *Parish Priests,* 249.

mestic chaplains, who daily performed mass in the private chapels. There were altar lights. A law of Edmund directs that a priest shall not celebrate without a light, not for use, but as a symbol. At low mass, one candle on the Gospel side of the altar was regarded as sufficient. More often two wax candles were placed on the altar, symbolizing Christ in His two natures, as Light of the world. An oil lamp was also bidden to be hung in front of the high altar in honour of the reserved Sacrament. A large ornamented wax light, called the Paschal Candle, was lit at Easter, and burnt through the Easter season. It symbolized the resurrection of our Lord. The lighting of the candles, it was written, was not to dispel darkness, but to show that the saints are lighted by the light of heaven.

Beside the ritual lights, it was customary to place torches at funerals about the bier, symbolizing the fact that the souls of the departed were in the land of light. It was customary, also, to place a chandelier in the church at the Purification of the Blessed Virgin Mary, and for the congregation to bring tapers with them. It was this custom that gave to the Feast of the Purification the title of Candlemas. The names of those departed belonging to the parish were read out in church, and the prayers of people asked for the repose of their souls. A custom which united the parishes together was to make an annual procession, if it was not too far, to the Cathedral, or mother church, carrying banners, and chanting or singing hymns. At Christmas, in addition to the Christmas services, there was often a grotto arranged in the church, with representation of the shepherds and the holy family.

On Ash Wednesday, there was an office for the signing of the people with ashes. The veiling of the rood took place at Passiontide. A procession, bearing palms, marched round the churchyard on Palm Sunday, and the Blessed Sacrament was taken from the high altar and placed on a special altar on Maundy Thursday, where it remained till Easter. Whitsunday was a time especially kept for baptisms, and the baptized were arrayed in white dresses, a symbol of baptismal purification. The fields were blessed on Rogation days. The festival of the dedication of the parish church was yearly kept. The Church in her services became thus the chief object of interest and the bond of the social life among the parishioners.

The devout priest of those times looked upon himself as the pastor of his people and the administrator of the sacraments. He had not on his shoulders the burden of a modern parish. The priest has now to keep up the various organizations associated with the modern parish, which make it like a great mill with its machinery, in comparison with the old handlooms that stood by the fireside. The priest of our time is so pressed with the burden of work that he gives less time to his own spiritual life than did the priest of old. The mediæval priest said the seven canonical hours in church. On Sundays and holy days, having finished Terce, he offered the Holy Sacrifice. Thrice in the year he heard the regular confessions of his people. Under some circumstances, mass was offered daily. There were those who, striving after greater holiness, would resort more frequently to the tribunal of penitence. There were few priests who did not have some sort of school for the children and communicants' class for the adults.

We are, however, obliged to note that there were some abuses and evil customs which sprang up in those days. People made the churchyard a place of general meeting, and used it for sports of a worldly nature, so that it was found necessary to prohibit them by canon. There were abuses by the Popes of putting foreigners, especially Italians, into English benefices for the purpose of taking the revenues.

Again, the evil of pluralities sprang up, and Bishop and clergy would hold the revenues of several benefices together. They would farm them out, taking the larger portion of the income for themselves.[14] This corrupt and worldly spirit indubitably tended to lower the spiritual standard of the clergy. What affected them perhaps still more was the endeavor to force celibacy upon them. It was found not possible to enforce the decrees which had been made on this subject. King Henry I. raised a large revenue by permitting the clergy to retain their wives, on payment of money for a license to do so. Many of the secular clergy argued that matrimony was a divine ordinance, whilst prohibition of it was only an ecclesiastical rule. It is well known that in the fifteenth century there were many ecclesiastics who had so-

---

[14] Cutts' *Parish Priests.*

called wives. Warham, the last Archbishop of Canterbury before the Reformation, is said to have had a wife, who was not secluded from the knowledge and society of his friends. Wolsey and Cranmer had women who stood to them in the same relation. This relation, however defensible, must have lowered the clergy's moral tone. Dean Colet, in his famous sermon preached at St. Paul's, 1511, before Convocation, sternly rebuked the faults of the clergy of his day. He dwelt upon their secularity, worldliness, and concupiscence. "They give themselves to feasts and banquetings; they spend themselves in vain babblings, they give themselves to sports and plays, they apply themselves to hunting and hawking. They drown themselves in the delights of the world." The bold, fearless words must be taken with some allowance. Many of these faults might be seen amongst the clergy of to-day.[15] We may believe that the standard of clerical life in England was higher than on the continent, and that on the whole, with the exception of concubinage, the clergy led moral lives.[16] There was nothing like

---
[15] *His. Ch. Eng.*, Wakeman, p. 165.
[16] *His. Ch. Eng.*, Wakeman, p. 165.

the prevalence of evil lives and ignorance of the clergy in the dioceses of the land that marked the advent there of Carlo Borromeo at Milan.[17] "Religion, then, in the Middle Ages," says Wakeman, "played a larger part in man's life than it does now. The large number of clergy enabled much more attention to be given to the wants of each individual soul than is possible nowadays." For those who could not read, rhyming paraphrases in English, to be committed to memory, were largely used. The Creed, the Lord's Prayer, the story of the Passion, the Ten Commandments, the Seven Deadly Sins, the principal festivals and fasts, were thus learned by heart by the ignorant. For the more learned who could read, and the rich who could buy, there was no lack of books. The primers were in the hands of every well-educated man or woman in the fourteenth and fifteenth centuries, and answered in no small extent to our Book of Common Prayer.

Thus in the Middle Ages, the Church, teaching her children either orally or by book, put them in possession of the seed-plot from which might grow the fairest forms of devotional life. By the

---

[17] *The Reformation*, Cazenove, p. 34.

creeds, she taught them the faith. In Holy Scripture, she pointed them to the basis of all meditation. In prayer, she trained them in the devotional life. By the Commandments and the list of the seven deadly sins, she led them to self-examination and penitence. By her public offices she taught them due harmony of praise, of intercession, and of prayer. Finally, in the weekly or daily Eucharist, she brought them to renewed self-consecration in the fulness of corporate worship." [18]

---

[18] *His. Ch. Eng.*, p. 184, Wakeman.

BOOKS REFERRED TO IN CHAPTER VII.

Documents of English Church History. Gee and Hardy.
History of the Church of England. Wakeman.
Latin Christianity. Milman.
Parish Priests. Cutts.
Social England. Traill.
History of the English Church, Fourteenth and Fifteenth Centuries. Capes.
Middle Ages. Hallam.

CHAPTER VIII.

THE REFORMATION IN ENGLAND.

WHATEVER view one may take of the Reformation, it is hardly possible to exaggerate its importance. It was like an avalanche, which was long preparing for its descent. It could but come; and a small event was enough to give it instant action. On the Continent, the immediate cause was the sale of Indulgences by Tetzel; in England, the King's divorce.

Christendom had already been divided into East and West, and the two portions had lived and grown separated from each other. In the West, the papacy had been moved to Avignon; subsequently, the papacy was restored to Rome. It descended from being an international representative, and became nationalized. At Avignon, it was a French power, and the mouthpiece of French policy; at Rome it became Italianized, and so continues to the present day.

The claims of the papacy had not been unquestioned in the Middle Ages. Marsiglio put forth a powerful book called *Defenso Parcis,* about the end of the thirteenth century, which denied that St. Peter had had any authority over the other Apostles, or had ever been proved to have been Bishop of Rome, or to have given the Popes a prerogative of government as Peter's successors. Wycliffe had attacked the iniquity of the Popes, and denied their right to rule. William of Ocham had contended that the Pope, even in discharge of his spiritual functions, was subject to the general voice of Christendom. At the Councils of Pisa and Constance, it was held that the Church in General Council was superior to a Pope, and could compel the Pope to obedience. The latter Council authorized a new election, after securing the deposition of two Popes and the resignation of one. In England, it was always maintained that the papal decrees were not binding, even on questions of faith and morals, unless accepted by the national authorities.

Again: the papacy had lost moral influence through the luxury and sensuality of the papal court. Its tyrannous greed, in demanding the first year's revenues of vacant bishoprics and other oppressive taxes, alienated both clergy and laity. This taxation was grievously felt by the laity in England; and prepared them for a revolt. As we have previously stated, the Pope had filled up a number of Sees with Italians, who never visited England, but drew their revenues. In Europe, the sale of indulgences aroused the moral indignation of the German people. It was not true that the indulgence gave to its holder the right to commit sin, but relieved him from the punishment of it, which is all the sinner usually cares about. The burning zeal of Luther shook the continent with opposition to such an immoral practice. In 1453, the fall of Constantinople, while it brought disaster to the Eastern Church, brought, through its fugitives, a reinforcement of classical literature into Europe. With the discovery of printing, and the renewal of classical learning, many had become fascinated with the old pagan life. The discoveries of the New World filled men with a spirit of enterprise, and made their hearts beat with a golden vision of conquest and wealth.

Popes themselves felt its influence. We read of a Pope who, pointing to a pile of gold coin, said, "You see what this fable of Christianity brings us in." These were some of the precedent causes of the great forward movement which we call the Reformation.

The further rent in Christendom caused by the Reformation could not take place, however, without much harm, whatever blessing might come with it. As Wakeman says, "In the Church, division, however we may palliate it, is, after all, sin, and carries with it its consequence of sin." The fact of the divisions of Christendom has been amongst the great hindrances to the effective representation of the Gospel. While a reformation was necessary, a division might have been avoided. The Church, herself, had earnestly demanded a reform. The call had been reinforced by committees of cardinals, who demanded a reform; both in the head and in the members of the Church. As the papacy would not lead in the way of reform, it had to come in other ways. Looked at in its political aspects, the Reformation was a part of a great general movement towards liberty, freedom, and the better government of mankind.

In England, the movement began under Henry VIII. and his parliament, as a political one. There were antecedent causes, as we have seen, but the king's matrimonial scheme was the match that touched the magazine and caused the explosion. In England, on its religious side, it was a removal of erroneous accretions of doctrine, and so a reformation, not a revolution.

On the Continent, it had first of all a religious aspect. It was a revolt against the immorality of the papacy and the sale of indulgences. It was also a gospel desire for justification by a living faith, in place of a formal observance of sacramental ordinances. In England, the Church, expressing her mind through her convocations, passed, in 1534, a resolution that "the Bishop of Rome hath not by Scripture any greater authority over the Church of England than any other foreign Bishop." It thus denied anew, what it had denied ever since the time of the Conquest, that the Pope had a supremacy, spiritual or temporal, over the Church of England, in virtue of anything declared in Holy Scripture. This was made effective by Act of Parliament, forbidding all appeals from English courts to the papacy.

The Divorce.

Here we may observe why the King was personally interested in the passing of measures restrictive of the papacy. It was necessary for the king's purposes to secure an acknowledged legal separation from Queen Catherine. He had been told by Cranmer, who was an ecclesiastical canonist, that he had a good case. "It would have to be legally presumed," Cranmer said, "whatever Catherine herself, as an interested party, might say, that her marriage with his brother Arthur was consummated." Consequently, the marriage with Henry, being against the Divine Law, according to the opinion of most theologians, could not have been allowed by the Pope. A former Pope, Innocent III., had said that "in decrees prohibited by Divine Law a dispensation cannot be given." The Pope had, however, undertaken to dispense this marriage, for Catherine had a bull in which the Pope had granted permission for her marriage with Henry, though perhaps her marriage with Arthur had been consummated. The Pope had thus undertaken to do what most theologians held was beyond his power. The papal dispensation for Henry's marriage to Catherine, therefore, being invalid, the marriage was not merely voidable, but "void," *ab initio*. Cranmer stated that this judgment would be the decision of the court. But what was to be guarded against was Catherine's appeal to the Pope, who would be bound to hear the case; for he, being under the control of Charles V., the German Emperor, uncle of Catherine, would reverse the English decision. Thus Henry, through his parliament, reaffirmed the old laws of the kingdom, which forbade all appeals to the Pope. Therefore, while a great and cruel injustice was done to Queen Catherine, the Church and nation thereby recovered their national rights and pre-Norman independence.

Some Romans have tried to prove the Pope in this matter the upholder of the sanctity and indissolubility of marriage. Here we quote from Brinckman: "But, while Clement gave his legates a special commission in the form of a decretal, in which he declared the marriage of Henry and Catherine null and void, and authorized them to give judgment for the king and notified the king by a Papal Brief what he had done in the matter, the Pope at the same time gave the legates *secret instruction* to burn the decretal letter embodying the commission, and charged them on no account to act upon it." [1] However badly the king, and all the parties concerned, came out of this miserable business, the Pope himself is far from being blameless.

THE CHURCH'S CONTINUITY.

There are some popular errors in regard to the Reformation to be noted. It is a habit of Roman controversialists to say the "Church of England was founded by Henry VIII." That is an historical misstatement that dies hard, but is, nevertheless, untrue. "Nothing," says the great historian, Professor Freeman of Oxford, "was further from the mind of either King Henry VIII. or Elizabeth. Neither of them ever thought for a minute of establishing a new Church." [2] Queen Elizabeth, in a letter to a Roman Catholic Princess of Europe, asserted that "there was no new faith propagated in England; no new religion set up but that which was com-

---

[1] *Anglican Brief*, p. 308: *Catherine of Aragon*, Froude, 67, 69, 84, and 85.
[2] *Disestablishment and Disendowment*, Freeman, 21-26.

manded by our Saviour, practised by the primitive Church, and approved by the Fathers."[3] Archbishop Bramhall thus expressed our position: "We do not arrogate to ourselves a new Church, or new religion, or new orders. Our religion is the same as it was, our Church is the same, our Holy Orders the same." The administrative power of Rome was in the king's way, and he swept it aside; but at heart and in religion he was a Roman Catholic. He had persons burnt for not believing in transubstantiation. He died, leaving a will providing for masses to be said for his soul.

Another popular error is that the Reformation under King Henry was a casting off of the Catholic Faith, and the adoption of what is popularly known as "Protestantism." Protestantism is both schismatical and heretical. It rejects Church authority and the Gospel's sacramental system. Mr. Gladstone said: "I can find no trace of the opinion, which is now common in the minds of unthinking persons, that the Roman Catholic Church was abolished in England at the period of the Reformation and that a Protestant Church

---

[3] *Life of Queen Elizabeth*, Camden, Book 1, p. 32.

was put in its place. The Church of England is the same Church that existed from the beginning. There was no new Church created and endowed by King Henry."[4] Sir Robert Phillimore, a noted legal authority, said: "It is not only a religious, but a legal error, to say that a new Church was introduced into the realm at the time of the Reformation. It is no less the language of our law than our divinity that the old Church was restored, and not a new one instituted."

Again, it is sometimes ignorantly asserted that the Church separated from Rome. Now we did not separate from Rome, but Rome separated from us. The Church before the Reformation was always known as the *Ecclesia Anglicana,* or the Church of England. She continued to exist at the Reformation as the same identical Church as she was before. No division took place during the period of the reigns of Henry VIII., Edward VI., and Mary. The people all, whatever their views, worshipped together as one Christian body. But in 1570, the Pope, excommunicating Queen Elizabeth, called on his followers to leave the old Church. Some did so, and it was not until 1854,

---

[4] *The State in Its Relation to the Church,* p. 127.

nearly three hundred years later, that the Romans were organized into dioceses. This schismatical body is commonly known as the Italian Mission. "We are a new mission," says Father Humphreys, S.J., "straight from Rome" (Humphreys' *Divine Teacher,* p. 54).

Thus we see how the Anglican Church, while rejecting the papacy, holds the ancient faith, essentially the same as it was held in Apostolic times; and by the Celtic, the Saxon, and the Eastern Churches and undivided Christendom. The Church, in all that she did in England, asserted that her members were Catholics—she was maintaining the Catholic Faith. Thus, in the statute passed, the twenty-fifth of Henry VIII., it was denied that the sanction of the Pope was essential to the validity of the consecration of Bishops and to the valid celebration of the sacraments. But this denial was based on the verified, historical fact that "divers Archbishops and Bishops have heretofore in ancient times been so consecrated, and they asserted that they were as obedient, devout Catholics, and humble children of God, as any people within any Christian realm,"

The Reformers and Their Principles.

There is a great diversity of opinion amongst partisans concerning the character and the motives of the reformers. They differed amongst themselves. But they have passed to the judgment seat of God, and the duty is not imposed on us of passing judgment on them. It is both wise and charitable to avoid exaggerated expressions. All that Anglican Churchmen are practically concerned with is the work they accomplished and the avowed principles of their action.

In the reforms she made, history shows that the Church appealed for her guidance to the Holy Scriptures, as interpreted by the Fathers, and the ancient Councils, and sought to maintain the faith as it had been held in the Church from the beginning. She appealed thus to Holy Scripture as corroborated by tradition. The Convocation of 1571 declared that "the clergy should never teach anything to be believed by the people but what is agreeable to the doctrine of the Old and New Testament, and collected out of that very doctrine by the *Catholic Fathers and ancient Bishops.*" No new Church was founded. "The continuity of the

Church," says Aubrey Moore, in his very able work, "was as true and real as the continuity of the nation."

I.—CATHOLIC DOCTRINE.

On its religious side, the movement did not begin with favoring Protestantism. In 1529, when the movement is said to have originated in the Reformation Parliament, as it was called, Convocation forbade the circulation of the works of Wycliffe, Knox, Luther, Zwingli, and the English Tyndall. The only authoritative doctrinal formularies put forth in King Henry's reign were the Ten Articles and a book called *A Necessary Doctrine and Erudition for Any Christian Man*. This book was put forth in 1543, by the authority of Convocation. It set forth the Creed, the Seven Sacraments, the Decalogue, the Lord's Prayer, the Hail Mary, and the four articles of Justification, good works, and prayers for the departed. It held the doctrine of the Real Presence, and the Sacrament of the Altar, and the validity of receiving it in one kind, and the duty of fasting Communion.

In the reign of Edward VI. we have the first Prayer Book put forth. It was drawn up by a commission consisting of an Archbishop, six Bishops, and six Doctors of Divinity. It had the authority of parliament and the Church. It "was accepted by Convocation," as Bishop Stubbs remarks. It was not a new book, but one composed out of materials previously existing. These were the old Service Books, including the rites necessary for the other Sacraments, as well as the Holy Eucharist; the Pontificale, containing the Ordinal, and others. In this Prayer Book of Edward VI., the Holy Communion was called the Mass. The words of administration were the first sentence of the present form. This was meant to mean a recognition of the Real Presence. The ancient ritual was practically unchanged. The priest wore the Eucharistic vestments, which symbolized the ancient Eucharistic doctrine. By the ordinal the three orders of Bishops, priests, and deacons were continued. The power to ordain or consecrate was shown to lie with the Bishops, who alone could give valid orders. The Anglican Church, in the interests of the Faith, recast her ordinal. It was with the intention, as is seen by the office itself, to hand on that divine succession of an Apostolic ministry and priesthood, which she believed her Bishops and orders then possessed.

About this time was put forth what is commonly known as "Cranmer's Catechism." It was a translation, and is chiefly noticeable as showing what Cranmer's views were at this time. It is the latest expression of them. The Real Presence, the Power of the Keys, and the Apostolic Succession are all plainly affirmed. We may omit dwelling on the later four years of Edward's reign, at which period there was an influx of foreign Protestants, whose object was to conform the doctrines of the Church of England to the sects of Zurich and Geneva. They effected, however, very little. But it was under their influence that a second Prayer Book was compiled. It is a comfort to find, however, that "this Prayer Book never had the slightest claim to ecclesiastical authority." It cannot even plead acceptance by the Church, for it was only in force about eight months, and probably it was never used at all in many parts of England. It was one of the most signal blessings of God on the English Church that Edward VI., "the young tiger cub," was early taken away. The loving presence of God, watching over the Anglican Communion, thus preserved it in Catholicity.

230   THE LINEAGE OF

The Interlude.

Mary succeeded Edward, and the Church and nation were reconciled to the papacy. Then, after five years, Elizabeth succeeded, and in her time the Prayer Book was put forth by the Church's authority, and secured for ever to the Church the liturgy in the common tongue. This is one of the greatest blessings derived from the Reformation.

Consecration of Parker.

In Elizabeth's reign, the orders and the faith and the continuity of the Church were preserved. Cardinal Pole, who was Archbishop of Canterbury, was dead when Elizabeth came to the throne, and Matthew Parker was legally and validly consecrated as Archbishop. Roman Catholics, now ashamed of their attacks upon the fact of his consecration, have granted that, according to the register preserved at Lambeth, Parker was consecrated on December 17, 1559. We have full and minute accounts given in the Lambeth Register.

There was a foolish story started forty-five years after the event, by Romans, denying the fact of Parker's consecration, and which was known as the Nag's Head fable. It has of late years been apologized for and repudiated by Roman authorities.

In the *Civita Cattolica,* the organ of the Pope, we find it said, "Let us admit the falsity of the Nag's Head fable, and deplore its use as an argument to cast doubt on Anglican orders." Objections to the consecration of Parker on the part of Romanists have now ceased, and have been apologized for. There was no doubt of the fact of his consecration.

The Earl of Nottingham, a Roman Catholic and a relative of Parker's, declared that he was present at the service. "There are at least nine distinct contemporary official and authentic documents to prove it." [5]

Parker was consecrated by four Bishops— Barlow, Hodgkins, Scory, and Coverdale. Barlow and Hodgkins had been consecrated by the old Roman Ordinal. One of Barlow's consecrators was Clerk, Bishop of Bath, who in his turn derived succession from Italian Bishops. The king's mandate for Barlow's consecration is still in existence, and also it is of record that he was installed and enthroned in his See. He was in-

---

[5] *Anglican Orders and Roman Claims,* p. 29.

volved in many legal contests, and his being a Bishop was never questioned. Moreover, he took his seat and voted in the House of Lords, which he could not have done unless it had been certified that he had been consecrated. His consecration has been fully vindicated by Courrayer, Mason, Bramhall, Haddon, and Lingard. De Augustinis, of great renown as a modern Roman theologian, in the late Conference about Anglican Orders, said: "Barlow was unquestionably a true Bishop."

As for Scory, who was consecrated under the Edwardine Ordinal in 1551, he had conformed and acted in Mary's reign as Suffragan Bishop of London.[6] This would show that the Edwardine Ordinal was accepted by Roman authority as valid.

Through his consecration, Parker's succession is thus traceable up to Archbishop Theodore, who was consecrated (668) by Pope Vitalianus.[7] Mat-

---

[6] Bonner's *Register,* fol. 347, July 14, 1554.

[7] There were many other Archbishops of Canterbury consecrated by Popes or Cardinals: Theodore, at Rome, by Pope Vitalianus, A. D. 668. Northelm, at Rome, by Gregory II., 736. Lambert, at Rome, by Paul I., 763. Wulfred, at Rome, by Leo XIII., 803. Celnotus, at Rome, by Gregory VI., 830. Athelard, at Rome, by Adrian II., 863. Plegmund, at Rome, by Formosus, 891. Richard at Avignon, by Alexander III., 1174. Stephen Langton, at Viterbo, by Innocent III., 1207. Boniface at Lyons, by Innocent IV., 1244. John Peckham, at Rome, by Nicholas III., 1278. Henry Chichele, at Sens, by Alexander V., 1409.

THE AMERICAN CATHOLIC CHURCH. 233

thew Parker, in tracing thus his succession back to the Archbishop Theodore, also does so to that old Saxon succession whose Bishops united under Theodore.

Along with Matthew Parker, we must consider the case of Archbishop Laud, who was one of his successors. He not only received his consecration through the old Anglo-Roman line of Parker, but through the Irish line of Bishops. For at the time of Queen Elizabeth, some of the Irish Bishops conformed—all but two, it is said. The record is as follows: St. Patrick was Archbishop of Armagh in 432. Christopher Hampton, in 1613, was the ninety-second Archbishop from him. He consecrated the English Bishop Thomas Morton in 1616, Bishop of Chester, who consecrated John Howson, Bishop of Oxford, in 1619, who, in 1621, consecrated Laud.[8]

Laud also received the Episcopate through the modern or Italian line. Mark Anthony, Arch-

---

Robert Winchelsea, consecrated by Gerard, Cardinal of Sabina, 1294. Simon Mepeham, consecrated by Peter Cardinal Praeneste, 1348. John de Stratford, consecrated by Vitalis Cardinal Albano, as Bishop of Winchester, 1323. Thomas Bradwardin, consecrated by Bertrand, Cardinal of St. Mark, Archbishop of Embrun, 1349.

[8] Moore, *The Reformation,* p. 280; Macbeth, *Ireland and Her Church,* 166. 168.

bishop of Spalatro, Italy, joined the Church of England, and was appointed Dean of Windsor. He, with others, consecrated George Monteigne in 1617 as Bishop of Lincoln, who consecrated the Bishop of London in 1621, who consecrated Laud.

We have also seen how the Patriarch of Jerusalem in the sixth century consecrated St. David. This Welsh line became in 1115 united to the English Church under the Archbishop of Canterbury. William Murray, the Archbishop of Llandaff, was, with Archbishop Laud, a consecrator in 1634 of Bishop Wren of Hereford, and from Wren and Laud all our present English and American Bishops have their spiritual descent. Our Anglican Episcopacy is thus derived from Roman, Irish, Welsh, and Eastern sources, the validity of whose orders has never been disputed.

In the consecration of Matthew Parker, it is of record that all four Bishops laid on their hands, and invoking the Holy Ghost, all said the words of consecration, the order being designated in the service. Thus the four acted as co-consecrators. This shows the great care that was taken to validate their action.

The matter and form of Parker's consecration as attested by the ancient liturgies was valid. Our Lord had given no one form as He had in respect of the sacrament of Baptism. There was no one form that had been universally used in the Church. The Roman ordinal was obscure, and it could not be told with certainty when the ordinand was ordained priest. It was therefore within the rights of the National Church, having expressed her intention to *continue the orders* as they anciently were, to improve her ordinal. She preserved in it all that was necessary for the conveyance of orders. There was the laying-on of the Bishops' hands, with the designation in the service of the order to be conveyed, and with prayer and invocation of the Holy Ghost. The intention of the consecrators was to do that which the Church proposed to be done. This is all that Cardinal Bellarmine says is necessary. The Church in her preface to her ordinal explicitly stated that her intention by it was that the ancient orders should be *continued*. The consecrators could not, by their own private opinion, if they had any, alter the intention of the Church of which they were the agents. Moreover, as de Augustinis held, "It is not necessary for the minister to intend to produce the *effect or end* of the sacrament, but only to do what the Church orders to be done." Thus the consecrators had a right intention, and the matter and form were correct.

As to Matthew Parker's jurisdiction, like all other Bishops, habitual or potential jurisdiction is conveyed by the consecration. Actual jurisdiction is the limitation of that which is inherent by consecration, and it limits the exercise of spiritual powers to certain places and over certain persons. It is regulated by canon law. This right to exercise Episcopal authority in a certain locality, or over certain persons, flows back on the death of its Bishop into the See, subject to the confirmation of the Bishops of the Province, or, in the case of an Archbishop, it goes to his comprovincials. On Elizabeth's succession there were nine Bishops who were in *canonical* possession of their Sees, and all these, except two, accepted Matthew Parker as their Archbishop. None of the uncanonically intruded Marian Bishops made any formal protest. So Parker's jurisdiction was confirmed.

We Anglicans know that we are possessed of orders, and real sacraments, and therefore have a true priesthood. The truth of our orders rests not only on an historical argument, but on their spiritual effects. Their enlightening power and saintly-making efficacy demonstrate to us, their recipients, their validity. When the Pope lately denied the validity of our orders, he declared what we know with divine certainty to be untrue, and proved he was not infallible.

Worship and Ceremonial.

The English Church thus preserves the Priesthood, the three Holy Orders, the ancient Faith as set forth in the Creeds and in the undisputed Councils. She preserved the ancient worship and ceremonial, which the Ornaments rubric of 1661 authorizes. As we of the American Church are not very familiar with this rubric, we here quote it in full: "And here it is to be noted that such Ornaments of the Church and of the Ministers thereof at all times of their ministration, shall be retained and be in use, as were in this Church of England by the authority of Parliament, in the second year of the reign of King Edward VI."

It is to be remarked that this rubric was not merely the republication of a former rubric; but by the introduction of new words it has the legal character of a new law, the legal effect of which, as Justice Coleridge said, was to "wipe out all the intervening legislation, and to establish for the Church's Ornaments those which were legalized at the time specified."[9] These were the Eucharistic vestments of amice, alb, girdle, stole, chasuble, surplice and cope for priests; and mitres and other regalia for Bishops; and the use of lights on the altar, and incense, etc. Thus the Ornaments Rubric provided for the use of the old ceremonial. We know that Queen Elizabeth had on the altar in her private chapel a silver crucifix, candlesticks, images of St. Mary and St. John. There were also a surpliced choir, priests in copes, and Eucharistic vestments were worn by her chaplain; also the great Bishop Andrewes, in his own chapel, used the same. The Anointing of the Sick, according to the injunction of St. James in the New Testament, was provided for in the First Prayer Book of Edward VI. The Rubric reads thus: "If the sick person desire to be anointed, then shall the priest anoint him upon the forehead or breast, making the sign of the cross; and we pray that

---

[9] *Hierugia Anglicana,* Part I.

God may restore him to bodily health, and release him from all troubles and diseases both of body and mind." In the book, by V. Staley, *Hierugia Anglicana,* we can see how these usages were continued in subsequent times.

DOCTRINE OF THE REAL PRESENCE.

The Church was no less careful in preserving the ancient doctrine of the Real Presence of Christ in the Holy Eucharist. There had been some question in the Church as to the right interpretation of her formularies. The Zwinglian theory that the communion was but a memorial service had obtained but little acceptance, yet the Calvinistic theory had received some encouragement. Calvin, having lost the priesthood, was compelled to assert that consecration was unnecessary, and he held consistently that the elements were not changed into the Body and Blood of Christ. They were only set apart, he affirmed, as holy things. On the delivery of them to the faithful believers, Christ's Body and Blood were, however, simultaneously given to them. The Presence depended thus upon the faith of the receiver, not on the consecration by the priest. This teaching is known as the theory of Reception. It is technically called virtualism.

Calvin's theory had been contradicted, however, by the 28th Article of Religion, which said that the "Body was given and taken and eaten in the Supper, after a heavenly and spiritual manner." If Christ be not in the Priest's hands as he holds the consecrated bread before the communicant, and says, "This is My Body," how can he be said to *give* the Christ? And if Christ be not in the communicant's hand as he receives that from the priest, how can he be said to *take* Christ? It was because Christ was present in the Sacrament by virtue of the consecration that the communicants were bidden to leave their seats, to come forward and kneel down, and in that posture of devotion receive the Sacrament. But questions arising, the Church herself pronounced judgment upon the opposing theories and condemned Zwinglianism and Calvinism. This she did officially by making additions to her Catechism in the year 1604; the last portion of the Catechism, on the Sacraments, being written by Bishop Overall, whose belief in the Real Objective Presence of Christ in the Sacrament is well known.

In the Catechism it is stated that baptism is an "outward and visible sign of an inward and spiritual grace given unto us." Baptism is an act which consists thus of two parts. The Sacrament of the Lord's Supper has three things said of it. First, it is an outward and visible sign, and secondly an Inward Thing, which is the Body and Blood of Christ, which are verily and indeed received by the faithful, and thirdly, a grace which follows faithful reception. The difference between Baptism and the Lord's Supper is, that in Baptism there is no necessary consecration of the element, or change made in respect of it; whereas in the Blessed Sacrament a change takes place, so that the Body and Blood of Christ, which is the inward part or Thing, is given by the priest and taken by the faithful. Thus the Church herself pronounced that her doctrine was that which is called the "Real Objective Presence of Christ."

And here we would reverently make a statement which may help souls to realize this great mystery of Christ's Presence. The unfortunate blunders and mistakes theologians have been led into have come in a large measure from arguing about the Presence in the Sacrament as if it were something taking place in the ordinary natural material order of things. It is an action on Christ's part which takes place in the spiritual organism of the Church, and is governed by laws of its own. Christ stands in the midst of His Church ever present to all the members of it. He does not have to move locally in order to manifest Himself in any portion of His Mystical Body. "Our Lord," says Cardinal Newman, declaring the present Roman doctrine, "neither descends from Heaven upon our altars, nor moves when carried in procession. The visible species change their position, but He does not move. We can only say He is present, not according to the natural manner of bodies, but sacramentally. His Presence is substantial, spirit-wise, and sacramentally, an absolute mystery."

Christ, at the time of the Institution, took the elements into His hands, and gathered them into sacramental union with Himself. And now, ever present and standing in the Church, through His ministers who act as His agents, He does the same thing. This tremendous act of loving condescension demands from us an acknowledgment by worship: and our act of adoration has for its object, not the elements, but the divine Person.

As one proof that there was no denial of the Catholic Faith by the English Church at the Reformation, we note that out of nine thousand clergy who said Mass under Queen Mary, only some two hundred or two hundred fifty beneficed clergy refused to conform at the accession of Queen Elizabeth and the promulgation of the new Prayer Book. As at least a large number of these Marian priests conformed, we cannot suppose that there was anything in the new Prayer Book that they regarded as denying the Catholic Faith, or as making a new religion. It seems to be an historical fact that the Pope himself offered to accept the changes, and was willing to allow the use of the Book of Common Prayer, if Queen Elizabeth would only acknowledge his supremacy.[10] We see in all this how the Anglican Church, while rejecting the papacy, and rejecting it now more strongly than ever, since it has added new doctrines to its creed, holds the ancient Faith.

The Reformation began in 1529 and was not completed until 1662. It had two phases, one in

---

[10] *Elizabethan Clergy*, Gee. *Queen Elizabeth*, Camden.

respect of Rome, and one in respect of Puritanism.

The Church Repudiates Puritanism.

The Church, having thus met Romanism, had next to meet with Puritanism and Protestantism. There had arisen within the Church of England, largely derived from the Continent, Calvinistic opinions. These developed in the time of Cromwell into the Great Rebellion; and overthrew for a time the monarchy and the Church. The Puritan theological positions had been met by the Church's great theologians, Hooker, Andrewes, and Laud. When in power, the Puritans, displaying their true spirit, forbade the use of the Prayer Book, broke the stained-glass windows in the churches, stabled their horses in the old Cathedrals, removed the altars from their ancient eastward position and substituted tables in their place, around which they gathered in unseemly and irreverent fashion. They denied the authority of the Church, the power of the priesthood, and the sacraments.

God's providence again preserved the English Church and overthrew the intruders. In 1661 the restoration of the monarchy took place, and with it the revival of the Church. Perhaps never so able a body of Bishops came together as those who assembled after the Restoration and put forth the Prayer Book in its last revised form. But first, in order to be fair, they sought, if possible, to unite the nonconforming bodies and to restore them to the Church. Thus, in 1661, the Savoy Conference was assembled, consisting of twelve Bishops and twelve Protestant ministers. Baxter, who led the Protestant side, produced a rival Prayer Book of his own making, and demanded its acceptance as an alternate. These ministers also demanded the disuse of the word "priest" in the Prayer Book, and the permission to use extempore prayers at the discretion of the ministers. They asked that the observance of Lent and Saints' Days be abolished. They objected to the sign of the cross in Baptism and the ring in marriage. They required that the practice of kneeling at the reception of the Holy Eucharist be discontinued. They objected to the teaching of the baptismal service, which taught that each person so baptized was "regenerated." They demanded that the Ornaments Rubric should be abolished, so that the Eucharistic vestments, and lights on the altar, incense, and other ceremonials should no longer be permitted.[11] They demanded also that those who received Presbyterian ordination should be admitted as Church clergymen, without any further form of laying-on of hands by the Bishop. These Protestant ministers also asserted that the Church was not merely acting inexpediently but sinfully, in making the sign of the Cross, in allowing the wearing of surplices, in the kneeling at Communion, and the declaring those baptized to be "regenerate." It is obvious that if their demands had been accepted the Church of England would have been wrecked, and it could no longer have been a branch of the Catholic Church. The Bishops refused, in obedience to the divine trust they had received, to grant these revolutionary demands. The Prayer Book was thus reëstablished practically as we now have it. We cannot be too thankful to God's providence that in this critical time He so saved it, and that the Church was thus found loyal to Catholic doctrine and worship, in resisting the attacks of Protestantism.

FINAL REPUDIATION OF ROMANISM.

Not long after, through her Bishops, she re-

---

[11] *Catholic Brief*, Burnie.

THE SEVEN BISHOPS SENT TO THE TOWER. A. D. 1688.

sisted the political influence of the Roman Catholic King, James II., who sought to make her subservient to his purpose; and when, in 1688, the king commanded the Bishops to cause his declaration, which was to be a step towards the revival of Romanism, to be read from every pulpit, we know how the demand was met. Archbishop Sancroft summoned a conference of Bishops and clergy at Lambeth. The discussion lasted for a week. Legal advice was sought. Seven Bishops presented a petition to the king, stating that his declaration was founded on a dispensing power which had already been declared illegal. The clergy and laity of the Church stood unitedly behind the Bishops in defense of national liberty. The Bishops, as being guilty of a libel, were committed to the Tower. We quote the vivid description of their committal as given by Wakeman:[12] "Their passage to the prison was a triumphal procession. Never since the days of the Crusades had the stolid natures of Englishmen been so deeply moved. As their barge passed swiftly down the Thames, hundreds of sober citizens assembled on the river banks, and kneeling in the black mud,

---

[12] *His. Eng. Ch.,* p. 399.

craved their blessing and thanked God for their courage. On the 29th their trial began. The judges were divided in opinion whether their petition could be in law a libel or not. The jury, unable to agree, were locked up for the whole of the night. At 10 o'clock in the morning they came into court and gave their verdict, 'Not guilty.' In a moment broke out a scene of wild excitement, unparalleled in the history of English courts of law. The crowd within and without Westminster Hall broke into a frenzy of enthusiastic joy. Men fell upon each other's necks, and wept and shouted and laughed and wept again; and amid the cheers of men and the boom of cannon the humble heroes of the Church passed in safety to their homes."

Thus the Reformation was made secure in England, and the Catholicity of the English Church vindicated both against Rome and Puritanism.

BOOKS REFERRED TO IN CHAPTER VIII.

Epitome of Anglican Church History. Parry.
Social England. Traill.
Life of Wolsey. Cavendish.
Catharine of Aragon. Froude.
Historians and the English Reformation. Littell.
Reformation. Blunt.
Lectures on the Reformation. Aubrey Moore.
History of the English Church in Fourteenth and Fifteenth Centuries. Capes.
England Under the Tudors. Innes.
Monasteries. Dom Gasquet.
Lollardism. Gairdner.
Papacy During the Reformation. Creighton.
Elizabethan Clergy. Gee.
Defense of the Church of England Against Puritanism. Cazenove on *Reformation.* Reply to Littledale.
Marian Reaction.
Principles of the Reformation. Lendrum.
Studies on the Prayer Book. Luckock.
History of the Articles of Religion. Hardwick.
Articles of Religion. Gibson.
Thirty-nine Articles and Reformation. Tyrrell Greene.
Thirty-nine Articles. Bishop of Brechin.
Anglican Brief and Roman Claims. Brinckman.
Pope and Council. Janus.
Anglican Orders. Roman Priest.
Reformation Settlement. MacColl.
Hierugia Anglicana. Staley.
Catholic Brief Against Harcourt. Burnie.
Reformation and Modern Work. Lane.

CHAPTER IX.

DECADENCE AND REVIVAL.

The activity of the Church found in the reign of Queen Anne was followed by the decadent spirit which marked the eighteenth century. It was universal over Europe. It affected the Church everywhere. In France, it led on eventually to the overthrow of religion. In England, it began at an early period of the eighteenth century. From the year 1771 to 1850, Convocation, which was the English Church's legal assembly, was suppressed. It was not allowed to meet for the transaction of business, nor has it yet recovered the power of passing canons. The repression of this constitutional body had an evil effect on the clergy and laity. The clergy of Tory politics became, in many instances, Jacobites. The practical activity of the Church since the Restoration had been chiefly the

A MODERN ALTAR AND REREDOS.

work of High Churchmen. The Whig government of this period was determined, however, on their suppression. It was opposed to all their plans for Church progress. The scheme for appointing Bishops in the American colonies was abandoned. The erection of fifty new churches, which had been voted by Parliament in the reign of Queen Anne, was reduced on the accession of George I. to twelve. The Bishoprics were distributed to the followers of the Whig Ministry, chiefly for political services. The Cathedrals ceased to be centres of diocesan activity. The spirit of the age was a rationalistic one. "The eighteenth century," says Liddon, "was marked by shallow common sense." It showed itself in France in the encyclopædistic teaching and the infidelity of Voltaire. This spirit of unbelief was checked in England by the great Bishop Butler and others. Their effort was to show the reasonableness of Christianity and to prove that it was agreeable to common sense. Butler's great book of the *Analogy,* edited of late by Gladstone, is still of value. The Church as a whole, at this period, was cold and its teaching rationalistic. The living and present Christ seemed to be left out of its theology. The necessity of conversion was not brought home to the people. Enthusiasm or zeal was repressed. The Archbishop of Canterbury warned Heber, setting out on his glorious missionary work for India, to put down enthusiasm. It was, we read, "an age of artificial formality, of self-satisfied enlightenment, of material prosperity, and lethargy." Like a malarious fog, it crept into the Church and laid its cold hand upon her heart. But the good Providence of God did not abandon her. God raised up Wesley, a High Church Evangelical, who preached with the effectiveness of a John the Baptist.

It was at the beginning of the nineteenth century that there arose a body of earnest, evangelical teachers. They preached the neglected doctrine of Christ's Atonement, man's lost condition, the necessity of conversion, and dependence for salvation on the merits of Christ. But their theology was deficient in not recognizing fully the Church and her Sacraments. The chief promoter in this work was the Rev. H. Venn, who was ordained in 1747. He was a moderate Calvinist, and election and predestination entered into his teaching. He ignored the baptismal grace of membership with Christ. Other popular preachers were John Newton, a rough converted sailor; Charles Simeon, a Cambridge man; Thomas Scott, and Joseph Milner. Amongst laymen, William Wilberforce added his great name and genius to this school. Hannah More, the friend of Dr. Johnson, was also an associate. Cowper, the melancholic poet, aided in the Olney hymn book, which was to the Low Churchmen what *Hymns Ancient and Modern* has been since to the Church.[1] The school was not noted so much for its scholarship as for its earnestness in preaching Christ. It did a good work. It had a number of lovely and holy men of an Evangelical spirit, like Fletcher of Madeley. As it gained political influence, it decreased somewhat in its spirituality. And it lastly passed into a phase of antagonism to certain Church principles set forth in the Prayer Book.[2] The condition of the Church buildings was at this time most deplorable. Sir Beresford Hope thus describes it: "The aisles were utilized by certain family pews or boxes, raised aloft, and approached by private doors or staircases. The pulpit stood against a pillar, with a reading-desk and clerk's box beneath. This was

---

[1] *Annals of the Low Church Party,* Proby.
[2] *Ibid.*

usually called the three-decker arrangement. There was a decrepit western gallery for the choir, and the nave was crammed with cranky pews of every shape. The whitewashed walls, the damp stone floors, the high, stiff pews, with faded red curtains, alloted to all the principal houses and farms in the parish, the hard benches without backs, pushed into a corner or cumbering the aisles, where the poor might sit, spoke eloquently of the two prevailing vices of the times, apathy and exclusiveness. The grand old fonts were frequently removed to the rectory garden to serve as flower pots, while their place was supplied by a small stone basin standing on a pedestal in some remote corner of the church. In the place where once the Holy Altar stood, vested in fair array, was to be found a mean table with a moth-eaten cloth upon it." [3]

This decadent condition, both in respect of the Church's teaching and worship, together with the suppression of a number of Bishoprics in Ireland, led, under God's guidance, to the rise of a school whose object was the recovery of the Church's Catholic heritage. We will treat of it now under

---

[3] *Pusey and the Church Revival,* Bp. Grafton.

two heads: its development in England, and in America.

The Movement in England.

It was heralded in England by Keble's famous sermon at Oxford, in 1834, on the Church's Apostacy. A number of holy and learned men became associates with him, among whom were Pusey and Newman, Isaac Williams, Harold Froude, Charles Marriot, and others. They began by putting forth a series of papers, which were known as "Tracts for the Times." These attracted universal attention, and were sold by the thousand. They began by teaching the almost forgotten doctrine of the Apostolic Succession, and of the Church as a divinely founded society. They brought out in their teaching the doctrine of the Incarnation, as the fundamental truth of Christianity.[4] It was in and through union with Christ as the second Adam that the new and redeemed race was being formed. Christ had ordained Sacraments, as channels of grace by which the union was begun and perfected. They did not deny anything the Evangelicals had previously taught, but thus supplemented their teaching. Their work was, however, violently

---

[4] *The Incarnation*, Wilberforce.

opposed. The Bishops, who at that time were mostly Low Churchmen, charged against them. The common people, who were inflamed by the cry of Romanism, began mobbing them. Anything seemed to be an excuse and an incitement to violence. The preaching in the surplice was one of these causes. Mobs assembled for weeks on Sundays at St. George's in the east of London, and with howlings and imprecations silenced the preacher. The Rev. John Mason Neale, the saintly founder of St. Margaret's Sisterhood, introduced at the funeral of one of the Sisters a bier, covered with a pall, on which was a cross. The mob, taking it for a sign of popery, attacked his house and tried to set it on fire.[5]

The movement, which had taken root, was checked about the year 1844 by the defection of Newman. He had been originally a Low Churchman, had accepted the *via media* theory, and became a High Churchman. He became convinced that the Decrees of Trent and the Thirty-nine Articles were reconcilable, and wrote Tract XC. in proof of this. Being of a very sensitive temperament, he felt wounded by the attacks made on him

---

[5] *Letters of the Rev. J. M. Neale.*

at Oxford, and in soreness of heart seceded to Rome. He endeavoured to defend his action by a theory of development, which was not altogether cordially received by the Roman Church. He was unlike Dr. Pusey, who had been from childhood grounded in the Church's doctrines, and who accepted the Faith as it had been received from the beginning, and proclaimed by the undivided Church. The secession of Newman and his friends only temporarily checked the movement for the recovery of the Church's heritage. The movement was not of man, but of God, and it went on.

Not long after another event happened, which began the contest with the State. A Rev. Mr. Gorham had denied the doctrine of baptismal regeneration as expressed in the Prayer Book. The Bishop of Exeter had refused to institute him. On appeal to the State Court, Gorham was sustained. It is said the Court, in doing this, put into his mouth a doctrine that he did not hold. The Bishop of Exeter summoned a synod of his clergy, which upheld the Bishop and the doctrine of the Church.[6] The Church's doctrine was thus

---

[6] *Privy Council Judgments*, Brooke. *Gorham v. the Bishop of Exeter*.

vindicated. In March, 1860, the English Church Union was formed.[7] Its objects were to defend and maintain unimpaired the doctrine and discipline of the Church of England, to afford counsel and protection to all persons, lay or clerical, suffering under unjust aggression, or hindrance in spiritual matters. This society, of which Lord Halifax is the president, consists now of four thousand clergy and thirty-eight thousand laity, and has done a noble work in safeguarding the Faith. At the beginning, the movement at Oxford was chiefly an intellectual and spiritual one. But as the movement extended, there went along with it the recovery of the Church's worship. "There was no practical difference," said Pusey, "between us and the Ritualists. We taught through the ear, and they taught also through the eye." Acting on the authority given by the Ornaments Rubric, lights on the Altar, vestments for clergy, the mixed chalice at the Eucharist, the eastward position at the Consecration, and other incidental ceremonials, were introduced. The Low Churchmen, who had failed to put down the move-

---

[7] *History of the Eng. Ch. Union*, Roberts, p. 12.

ment through the charges of the Bishops, now resorted to legal efforts.

A Low Church Association was formed for the prosecution of High Churchmen, and a considerable sum of money was raised. Civil suits to put down ritual were instituted. The civil court of last resort then existing was that of the Privy Council. It was reported by Lord Brougham that, by a mistake in 1830, ecclesiastical causes had been assigned to it. It was not a court composed of permanent members, but, being appointed from time to time, was under the manipulation of political influences. This packed and prejudiced the tribunal. A number of ritual cases were tried before it. Amongst them was that of the reredos of St. Paul's Cathedral. The decisions were not always consistent with one another, but they were marked by obvious prejudgments. On one occasion three of the judges would not be present at the formal decision, but one of them, Chief Baron Kelly, publicly declared the decision to be a political one.[8]

The Catholic clergy who were condemned, holding that a civil court had no power to decide spirit-

---

[8] *Privy Council Decisions,* Brooks.

ual causes, refused obedience. A number of them were sent to prison, and became martyrs to the Faith. The Rev. Mr. Tooth and others, like Daniel of old, went to prison rather than obey the king's decrees. They stood for the Church's freedom in spiritual matters from State control. Their sufferings and courage helped to deliver many of the English clergy from a false Erastianism. It taught them the solemn duty to disobey the state when its decrees conflicted with those of the Church. The great movement on behalf of the Church's emancipation and recovery of her heritage was thus aided by these adverse decisions. It moved on.

The Broad Church.

But now we are bound to mention the rise of a new school within the Church. Partly owing to German rationalistic speculations concerning the Bible, partly to the new methods of investigation, given to all subjects, by the discovery of the process of evolution; partly by the growing critical spirit of agnosticism, doubts were being cast on the inspiration of Scripture. The authenticity of the Old Testament writings and fundamental truths of Christianity were being questioned. This line of thought came to be known as the Broad Church School. One of its first efforts was the publication of a book called *Essays and Reviews*. Some of the writers appeared to deny the genuineness of the prophetic predictions, the reality of the miracles, the supernatural conception of the Son of God by the Blessed Virgin, the Resurrection of Christ's crucified Body. The Bishops, however, collectively condemned the book, declaring it to be unsound and dangerous. Another Broad Church leader, Bishop Colenso, put forth a book entitled, *The Pentateuch and Book of Joshua Critically Examined*. He questioned the veracity of the Pentateuch and also the divine authority of the Epistle to the Romans. The matter was finally taken up by his Metropolitan, Bishop Grey, of South Africa. Bishop Colenso was brought to trial, his book condemned, and he was removed from the Episcopate. This action was subsequently approved by the House of Convocation.

A Mr. Voysey, having published sermons in which the inspiration of Holy Scriptures, the Divinity of Christ, and the doctrine of Eternal Punishment were denied, the Archbishop of York took proceedings against him. While the English Church Union was willing to assist pecuniarily the Archbishop, and asked the Low Church Association to join with them, the Low Churchmen refused. They were willing enough to attack ritual, but not to join in defending the divinity of Christ. Mr. Voysey subsequently joined the Unitarian body.

In fairness to the Privy Council, it is to be stated that the Low Church Association failed in its attempt to secure a condemnation of the doctrine of the Real Presence. Mr. Bennett, the rector of Frome Selwood, had stated his belief in the "Real, objective Presence of our Lord, under the form of Bread and Wine, upon the Altars of our churches," and "whom myself adore, and teach the people to adore, Christ present in the Elements under the form of Bread and Wine." The Court acquitted Mr. Bennett, as not having gone beyond the allowed teaching of the Church.⁹ Flushed by their success before the civil tribunal, the Low Churchmen now attacked one of the Bishops. They selected Dr. King, the saintly Bishop of

---

⁹ *Privy Council Decisions*, N. 271. *His. Eng. Ch. Union*, 114-120.

Lincoln. This case, however, was held before the Archbishop of Canterbury, sitting with a number of Bishops as assessors. The Court met July 23, 1899. Celebrations of the Holy Eucharist were made in the morning by the High Churchmen throughout England, "that God might be pleased to overrule the trial to His greater glory and the good of His Church."

The points at issue were: The use of the mixed Chalice, its mixture during the service, the ablutions at the end, the eastward position in the early part of the service, and during the prayer of consecration, the singing of the *Agnus Dei* after the canon, lighted candles upon the altar, the sign of the holy cross by the Bishop in giving the Absolution and Benediction. In all these, save the trifling one of the Cross, the decision on Churchly and historical grounds was given in favor of the Bishop. Thus, after years of trial, a real victory was made on behalf of the Church cause.

Signs of Peace.

And now some efforts for peace began to be made. Archbishop Tait drawing near his end, sought a reconciliation with Fr. Mackonochie.

The bringing of Churchmen of all schools together in Church congresses began to lessen the bitterness of feeling. The attacks of political dissenters upon the Church drove Churchmen into a defensive alliance. The papal decision against our orders also helped on the growing spirit of union, and disillusionized the minds of many of the ritualists as to the spirituality of Rome. Round table conferences began to be held, where Low and High Churchmen met together to discuss their differences and find terms for agreement. The development of Religious Orders with their missionary spirit won for the High Church school great respect. The rise of St. Andrew's Brotherhood and the Laymen's Forward Movement have contributed towards unity. It is being recognized that the Catholic Movement in its doctrine does not deny the early Evangelical teaching, but only supplements it, and that the Church's recovered ritual has not been introduced in imitation of Rome, but as a recovery of her own heritage.

II.—The Church in America.

Let us now turn to the rise of the Church in America. Sir Walter Raleigh had attempted

THE AMERICAN CATHOLIC CHURCH.   265

in 1585 and 1587 to establish a colony in Virginia. He parted with his Letters Patent to a company of merchants, and presented to them a donation of £100, for the propagation of the Christian religion in Virginia.[10] Prayers were first read on the coast of the Pacific by the Rev. Francis Fletcher, which act is commemorated by a stone cross set up in the Golden Gate Park in San Francisco. In the East, Sir George Weymouth visited the coast of Maine, and set up a cross on Monhegan Island. There, in 1607, the Rev. Richard Seymour held a service. The Church was really founded in the year 1606 at Jamestown. In that year, King James I. chartered the Virginia Company. The territory thus granted extended from Cape Fear to the Bay of Fundy. The portion from Cape Fear to the Potomac was placed in charge of a number of persons residing in London, and so came to be called the "London Company." It is a matter of more than ordinary interest that one of its members was the Rev. Nicholas Ferrar, who founded the Religious House of Little Gidding in England. He and his holy household, whose history should be read by all Churchmen, must have often prayed

---
[10] *Title Deeds Ch. Eng.*, Garnier, p. 254.

for the work. While the enterprise was of a mercantile character, religion entered into it. The proposed colonists were instructed to make "Yourselves all of one mind for the good of the country and your own, and to serve and fear God, the Giver of all goodness; for every plantation which our Heavenly Father hath not planted shall be rooted up." We find the colonists on arriving preparing for the coming Sunday service by hanging up an old sail, fastening it to three or four trees. It was to serve as a shelter from the sun and rain. They made seats out of rough logs. They placed a bough of wood between two of the trees to serve them as a pulpit. Their chaplain was the Rev. Robert Hunt, a man of robust courage and earnest piety. Subsequently we read that Morning and Evening prayer was daily said. The low standard of Churchmanship was, however, marked by their having the Holy Communion only once in three months. The settlers had many severe trials with the climate and with the Indians. They were at one time famishing, and the colonists on the point of deserting the work, when Lord Delaware arrived with reinforcements. Lord Delaware knelt in prayer on the bank of the river, and all joined in thanksgiving to God for His mercy in saving them. The simple church which they had erected, and which had almost fallen to pieces, was repaired, and daily service was renewed. We have to record, however, that in 1609 a Dutch ship appeared, having for sale a cargo of twenty negroes. In this way, our evil system of slavery began. The administration of the colony, which was first under Presidents, in 1624 was placed under Governors, the first of whom was Lord Delaware. Before leaving Jamestown affairs, "it is a just pride," says John Fiske, "that the work of founding a university was proposed." If New England can rejoice in the founding of Harvard College, Virginia can rightly boast of the heroic endurance of her settlers and their provision for education.

THE CHURCH'S GROWTH.

The Church, which gradually grew in Maryland and Virginia, began a feeble existence in the North. The settlers of New England, who landed at Plymouth in 1620, were separatists from the Church. The Puritans, as is sometimes thought, were not advocates of religious liberty. Churchmen and Quakers were severely treated. We find in 1750, a Churchman, an old man, severely whipped for not attending meeting. The Charter granted to the Massachusetts colony had declared that its end was to win the natives of the country to the knowledge of the only one God and Saviour of mankind. But they treated the Indians as Amorites, Hivites, and Jebusites. In their war with the Indian tribe of Pequots, the colony adopted a policy of extermination. Robinson, their former pastor at Leyden, said to the Governor of Plymouth, "Oh, that you had converted some before you had killed any!" It may be gratefully remembered that John Elliot, formerly a minister of the Church, became the Apostle of the Indians. He translated the Scriptures into their tongue, and won many of them to Christ. The settlers who landed at Salem in 1630 were not separated from the Church. They called the Church of England their "dear Mother," acknowledging that the hope and part they had obtained in the common salvation, "they had received in her bosom and suckled from her breast."[11] Five ships brought over two hundred and fifty settlers. At Salem, their spiritual leader was the Rev. John White, who had two

---

[11] *Ch. in America*, Hodge, p. 57.

Church ministers with him. Dr. Lake, the Bishop of Bath and Wells, gave the enterprise its blessing. In 1641 the Rev. Richard Gibson had a church and a parsonage at Portsmouth. The Rev. Robert Radcliffe held service in the old South Meeting House in Boston, and aroused much resentment by officiating in his surplice and using the Book of Common Prayer. The Rev. Eland Evans ministered for some eighteen years in Christ Church, Philadelphia. He is said to have baptized several hundred Quakers, and was by that body bitterly disliked. In New York, the Church was more favorably received. In 1697, Trinity Church having been founded, the Rev. William Vesey was called to be its rector. St. Mary's Church was founded in Burlington in 1703, St. Peter's Church in Albany, 1716. A memorable event in 1722 took place in New Haven.[12] About 1711, Yale College had received a present from England of 800 volumes for their library, among which were to be found works by divines of the English Church. The President of the College, Dr. Cutler, and two of his leading professors, Samuel

---

[12] Coleman's *Ch. in Amer.*, 40; Wilberforce, *P. E. Ch. in America*, 104; Hodges' *Epis. Ch. in Amer.*, p. 65.

Johnson and Daniel Brown, were led to accept the divine right of the Episcopacy. On the day after the commencement, 1702, the faculty of Yale College, with five prominent American pastors, presented to the trustees a letter stating their religious change of mind. They said they had become convinced of the invalidity of Presbyterian ordination. They felt they could not continue outside of visible communion of an Episcopal Church. They were dismissed from their post, hotly abused, and suffered in other ways much persecution. The conversion of these eminent Protestant ministers was a blow to Puritanism. "The Church" thereafter, we read, "progressed in Connecticut, being commended to the people by the solid attainments, the intelligent loyalty, and the elevated character of the clergy."

The Church's Weakness.

But during the colonial period the Church suffered under two great disabilities. It had no Bishops, and it was unpopular. The Episcopate had been urgently and often asked for from England, but for political and other reasons it had been refused. That the Church should have been kept alive in this marred condition of its government is a marvel. For ordination, candidates were obliged, with much expense and danger, to cross the ocean. The clergy who came from England were regarded by the colonists as foreigners. A laxity of discipline ensued, which makes the reading of clerical life, especially in the South, unpleasant and regretful. The loss of the enlightening grace of Confirmation showed itself in the ignorance of the Church's polity and a weakened spirituality. When, in the eighteenth century, English Churchmen were willing to give us Bishops, they were met by un-churchly American hostility. "They were not wanted." Again, the Church was very unpopular. The other religious bodies were possessed of a strong animosity against the Church. One Morton of Merrymount was accused of atheism by his neighbours of Boston, the charge being based, according to John Fiske, on the fact that he used the Book of Common Prayer.

"The Puritan opinions in politics and religion were violently opposed to civil and ecclesiastical order. To their minds," says Dr. Hodges, "the Church stood for the bigotry of Bishops and the tyranny of kings."

When we come to the American Revolution, we

find a number of the clergy, English by birth, siding with England. Some of them left their parishes and went back to the old country, or to an English colony. Their attitude of course increased the unpopularity of the Church. The use of forms of prayer was called unspiritual. It was said to be a quenching of the spirit, and the Church's worship was denounced as a cold formalism. Nevertheless it continued to grow.

Of the necessary changes in the Prayer Book, in consequence of our separation from England, we will treat later.

The Episcopate was eventually obtained from Scotland and England. The Church's progress was aided by the heroic lives of some of our missionary Bishops. Among these was the great Bishop White, a man of balanced wisdom and sanctity. Bishop Seabury, who had obtained his consecration from Scotland, and who was a devoted High Churchman, and Bishop Hobart of New York, who was like-minded in his teaching and a great administrator, left their marked impression on the Church. Bishops Chase and Kemper, who were great missionaries, planted the Church in the central and farther West.

The Catholic Movement.

As the Church grew, early in the nineteenth century there was a development here, under the guidance of God's Holy Spirit, of that same movement for the recovery of the Church's full heritage of doctrine and worship as had begun in England. The teachings of Hobart and Seabury laid the foundation of this recovery. Indeed, it has been thought by some that, as it was no imitation or echo of English teaching, they had led the way.

They taught the doctrines of the Church, the Apostolic Succession, Baptismal Regeneration, and the Prayer Book, as the Church's Rule of Faith. The teaching of some High Churchmen on the subject of the Holy Eucharist was very strong. In a note to his famous sermon preached by the Rev. Samuel Farmer Jarvis, before the Bishops, clergy, and laity, constituting the Board of Missions in 1834, by the title, "Christian Unity Necessary for the Converting of the World," he said: "We have no right to banish from our Communion those whose notions of the Real Presence of Christ in the Sacraments rise to a *mysterious change* by which the *very Elements* themselves, though they retain their original properties, are corporeally united with, or transformed into, Christ."

The revival of Church teaching began here, as in England, to be opposed. The slightest revival of enrichment in the services was condemned. Many of the churches then had the old three-decker arrangement, consisting of a pulpit beneath which was a reading desk, and beneath that a place for the clerk, who said the responses. A recessed chancel was looked upon with abhorrence. Bishops insisted there should be nothing looking like an altar in the chancel. It must be an honest table with four visible legs. The introduction of flowers was sternly forbidden,[13] as was also a cross on the Holy Table. A cross having been placed on the wall over the altar in the Church of the Advent, Boston, the Bishop assigned it as a reason why he would not visit the Church for Confirmation.[14] A cross having been found in the chapel of the General Theological Seminary, on the front railing of the chancel, it was declared to be improper by the dean, and ordered to be removed.[15] Where there was a reading desk, where the prayers were said,

---

[13] *Appendix Gen. Conven,* fol. 249.
[14] *Life of William Croswell.*
[15] *Journal Gen. Convention,* 1844, Appendix.

it faced the people. On one occasion, when the venerable Dr. Edson of Lowell was saying the office stall-wise, Bishop Eastman, who was present, rose and took him by the shoulders, and made him turn round facing the congregation. There were no lights on the altar, no vested choristers, no cross borne in procession. The clergyman preached, and sometimes said the whole service, in the black Geneva gown, and the Holy Communion was but seldom administered.

It is to be remembered that Miss Seton, a devout person, besought the rector of Trinity Church, New York, for more frequent celebrations. She was refused, and subsequently joined the Roman Communion, where she founded an order of the Sisters of Charity. In the forties, a meeting of some High Church clergy took place in New York, among whom were Dr. Muhlenberg and William Croswell of Boston, who discussed the possibility of having on every Sunday a celebration of the Holy Eucharist. There was much party spirit at this time. The Low Churchmen had many holy men among them, but some took here, as in England, to the tactics of persecution.

There was a young man at the General Theological Seminary by the name of Arthur Carey. He was a young man noted for his piety, and of considerable intellectual ability. He had adopted the opinion afterwards put forth by Dr. Pusey, that the decrees of Trent and our Thirty-nine Articles were capable, *by explanation,* of a reconciliation.

In 1843, at the time of his ordination by Bishop Onderdonk, the Rev. Dr. Smith and the Rev. Dr. Anthon rose and read a long protest, grounded on Carey's alleged doctrinal errors. Bishop Onderdonk, however, stated that the accusation had already been investigated, that there would be no changes in the service of the day, and that all the candidates present would be ordained. This brought Bishop Onderdonk into great disfavor with the Low Churchmen. He was himself the next object of their attack. They charged him with acts evincing a "prevalent impurity of mind." The evidence was imperfect,[16] and as the great Bishop Whittingham said in his written opinion, "The probabilities were strong against it." But the Low Church Bishops voted for his condemnation. It was obviously a mere party judgment.

---

[16] *Trial of Bp. Onderdonk,* published by the Court.

Bishop Onderdonk was suspended. Subsequently, in the same spirit, the great Bishop Doane of New Jersey was attacked. One charge related to money matters. His diocesan convention, clergy and laity, rallied to his support, and his masterful mind was able to defeat the attack.

In Massachusetts, the Rev. Oliver S. Prescott, at one time an assistant at the Church of the Advent, Boston, was presented for trial for erroneous teaching. Three trials took place. It was not proved that he had heard confessions, but that he had taught the right of every layman to resort to the Sacrament of Penance if he felt the need, and the priest, if he judged him penitent, to give him absolution. Prescott was condemned and suspended from exercising his priestly office until he should renounce his teaching. He was urged by counsel to appeal to the civil courts, being assured that they would grant relief in such an unjust sentence. But, unwilling to bring such matters before civil tribunals, he declined doing so. Eventually Bishop Whittingham of Maryland, saying, "What a Bishop could do, another Bishop could undo," invited him into his diocese, where he would be free from the sentence in which he had acquiesced.

A few years previously, 1844, a fierce attack had been stirred up against the General Theological Seminary. A series of some forty-three inquisitorial questions was addressed to its dean and professors. "What had been taught there concerning the errors of Rome? the authority of General Councils? whether the works of Pusey, Newman, Keble, and Palmer were privately recommended, or the Oxford Tracts? whether the errors of the Romish Church were duly exposed? What superstitious practices of the Romish Church, such as the use of the crucifix, etc., were adopted?" It appeared that, as a matter of Christmas decoration, a cross, ornamented in part by artificial flowers, was placed on the front railing of the chancel. This was made a comment by the dean. A great effort was made at General Convention to obtain from the Bishops a public condemnation of these errors in doctrine and practice, "having their origin, it was said, in certain writings emanating chiefly from members of the University of Oxford in England."

The effort, however, which took the form of a resolution, was voted down. The House of clerical and lay deputies, as giving a quietus to the agitation, resolved that the liturgy, "offices and articles of the Church were sufficient exponents of her sense of the essential doctrine of Holy Scripture, and that the canons of the Church afforded ample means of discipline and correction for all who might depart from her standard. And further," they declared, "the General Convention was not a suitable tribunal for the trial and censure of, and that the Church is not responsible for, the errors of individuals, whether they are members of this Church or otherwise."

THE ATTACK ON THE PRAYER BOOK.

Thus defeated, the Low Churchmen turned next to an attack upon the Prayer Book. It contained, they said, "Roman germs. It taught the doctrine of Apostolic Succession, Baptismal Regeneration, the priest's right to give absolution in private. It called the Holy Table an Altar, it upheld the doctrine of the Eucharistic Sacrifice." Now the basis of the sacramental system lies in the doctrine of baptism, as the effective instrument of regeneration. So clearly is the teaching of the Church expressed in her baptismal office, that it is a wonder any should not have admitted it to be so. Some had, however, invented an ingenious theory that regeneration was promised prospectively to a baptized infant, in virtue of the faith of the sponsors. But one, who was subsequently a Bishop of the Reformed Episcopal body, declared that in administering on one occasion baptism privately to a sick child, he perceived that no sponsors were required, but the Church went on to say that, "seeing this child is regenerated." His theory, he said, thus fell to the ground. The effort, however, to get the Prayer Book changed at the General Convention signally failed.

Upon this, a number of Low Churchmen, led by Dr. Cummins, Bishop of Kentucky, left the Church. Dr. Cummins said he had "lost all hope that the system now prevailing so extensively in England, and in the Protestant Episcopal Church, can or will be eradicated by any acts of the Church, legislative or executive." He left the Church, and was deposed by the House of Bishops.

The Holy Eucharist Controversy.

Next arose the controversy over the Holy Eucharist. Dr. de Koven had defended the doctrine of the Objective Real Presence as taught in the

Prayer Book and Catechism. Chosen to be Bishop of Illinois, his election was not confirmed. The movement, however, was not checked, but began rapidly to grow. A more developed ritual took place in certain churches, like that of St. Alban's, New York. Lights and vestments began to be introduced. The Cowley Fathers, coming from England in 1872, gave a great impulse to the Church spirit in Boston.

It was about 1874 that a further attack was made on ritual. It was sought to put it down by legislation. It was like the last fatal charge of the old Guard at Waterloo. The fears of many Churchmen had been excited by the cry of Romanism. Under the pressure of the excitement a canon was forced through General Convention which forbade any acts of reverence by genuflection or otherwise towards the Elements. Here, we may reverently say, God took part in the struggle. The Low Churchmen were victorious in getting their canon passed, but God had struck its authors with judicial blindness, for the way in which they defeated themselves can be explained in no other manner. The canon which was to forbid all acts of reverence and adoration only forbade them as offered to the *elements.* The canon omitted to state the *consecrated elements.* The canon never was put in operation and finally was repealed in Boston thirty years later. One misunderstanding may here rightly be removed. As the Jewish priest waved the offering before the Lord, so the Christian priest elevates the sacred elements, doing this as *offering them to God,* not, as is sometimes supposed, for the adoration of the people.

It is also necessary to notice that there arose some of the Broad Churchmen here, as in England, who denied the Virgin Birth of our Blessed Lord. The Rev. Howard MacQueary and Dr. Crapsey were tried and condemned.[17] The effort made to liberalize the Church and make it more like the Unitarian, while popular with the worldly minded, is not being well received by the orthodox and devout. Thus we see how the great movement on behalf of the recovery of our Catholic heritage in doctrine and worship has progressed, under God's good guidance, in our American Church.

The Changes in the Prayer Book.

One further matter must be touched upon.

---

[17] *Christian and Catholic,* Dr. Grafton.

After the separation from England, it became necessary that some changes should be made in the Book of Common Prayer. Our American Preface states that "when in the course of Divine Providence, these American States became independent with respect to civil government, their ecclesiastical independence was necessarily included." Alteration in the Liturgy became necessary in prayers for our civil rulers, and some other alterations were made. But it is declared that "the Church was far from intending to depart from the Church of England in any essential points of doctrine, discipline, and worship, further than local discipline should require."

It is important to note that this expressed intention gives us the rule by which all the changes are to be interpreted. It shows that mere omission would not mean rejection of either doctrine or practice. Thus, the Athanasian Creed was omitted from recitation, but remained as a true exposition of the Faith. The form of private absolution of the sick was omitted, but allowed to be given privately in a new office, the Visitation of Prisoners. The frequent repetition of the Lord's Prayer, to which some had objected, was obviated. Selections of Psalms were introduced, which allowed of the omission of the recitation of the imprecatory ones. The sign of the cross in baptism was made optional. The evangelical canticles of the *Benedictus, Magnificat,* and *Nunc Dimittis* were omitted. Even an Article in the Apostles' Creed, "the descent into hell," was bracketed. These concessions were made according to the request of sectarians, when union was sought in England between themselves and the Church. But they had no effect in America in diminishing the sectarian feeling of opposition. It only showed that concessions do not lead to union, but rather intensify sectarian pride and opposition. Our great Bishop Seabury allowed these changes, especially those in Morning and Evening Prayer. He left it, he said, "to a wiser generation to have them reinstated." In respect to the evangelical canticles, this has now been done. Seabury was willing to allow of these changes in the minor offices, provided that he could have the revision of the great office of the Holy Eucharist. He had been consecrated a Bishop in Scotland, and the Scotch Liturgy was far richer and more Catholic than the English one. The Scotch Bishops had requested

THE AMERICAN CATHOLIC CHURCH. 285

Seabury to adopt their Communion Office, and Bishop Seabury promised to do his best to induce the American Church to adopt it. The result has been that the American office is the most glorious Liturgy of all the Churches belonging to the Anglican Communion. We find, for instance, in the Institution Office the term "Altar." This term, save in the Coronation Service in England, was omitted in the English Book. The Holy Communion is also called in the Consecration office of a church, "the Blessed Sacrament of the Body and Blood of Christ." This it is well to remember, as there are those who have raised objections to the title "Blessed," being given to this Sacrament. It is, however, a Prayer Book definition and terminology. In the Institution Office, we find the Holy Communion called by its ancient name, "the Holy Eucharist." In this office also, in its prayer, we find it asserted that Christ has purchased to Himself an universal Church, and "has promised to be with the ministry of Apostolic Succession to the end of the world." The relation of the instituted priest and his people is called in the same office a "sacerdotal connection," and in the Visitation of the Sick, the minister, on behalf of all who are present, prays that "when we are gathered unto our fathers, it may be in the Communion of the Catholic Church."

More important, however, were the additions made to the Holy Communion consecration prayer, or canon, as it is called. The English book is deficient, herein, in an explicit invocation of the Holy Ghost. This, which is held as so important in the Eastern Church, is fully stated in our own Liturgy. In it "We pray Thee, Merciful Father, to hear us, and of Thy Almighty goodness vouchsafe to bless and sanctify with Thy Word and Holy Spirit, these Thy gifts and creatures of bread and wine, that we, receiving them according to our Saviour, Jesus Christ's, holy institution, in remembrance of His death and passion, may be partakers of His most blessed Body and Blood." It is to be noted here that the elements are not only called creatures, but, having been endowed with the sacramental gift by virtue of the Institution, are called "Holy Gifts," as well as creatures, having received the inward thing or gift of Christ's Body and Blood.

More liturgically important is the explicit statement and action that shows the Holy Eucharist is not only a Communion, but it is also a Sacrifice. It is one, we know, with that ever being presented on the Heavenly Altar, and a memorial re-presentation of the offering on Calvary. We make the oblation of the Sacrament, and offer it to God. So "we, Thy humble servants, do celebrate and make here before Thy Divine Majesty with these Thy Holy Gifts, which we *now offer unto Thee,* the memorial Thy Son hath commanded us to make." And this offering which we make and plead is stated to be for the "whole Church." We ask God to accept this our Sacrifice, "that we and all Thy *whole Church* may obtain remission of our sins, and all other benefits of His Passion." As previously, the priest had asked for prayers for the Church Militant, that is, the Church on earth; here, as the priest presents the great Memorial Sacrifice, he pleads it on behalf of the *whole Church.* Now the whole Church must include, not only those on earth, as the Church Militant does, but the faithful departed. So we profess in the hymn beginning, "The living and the dead, but one communion make." We may not know what the latter need, and so our Mother Church prays in general terms for all, "for forgiveness of sins, and all other benefits of Christ's Passion." This has been a great comfort and support to all who have lost dear ones who have gone before.

The special liturgical glory of the Anglican Church is her placing the *Gloria in Excelsis* after the Communion of the people. In the early liturgies, it stood at the beginning. The Liturgy which set forth the drama of the Incarnation and Christ's death, began then with the Song of the Angels at Bethlehem. But our Church placed it after the communicants had received. We were to sing it, as an act of worship and devotion, in the sacramental presence of our Blessed Lord. By this act she reserves the Blessed Sacrament, not for the purpose of Communion, but after Communion, for the purposes of devotion.

In respect to the attitude of the priest, the Bishops at the General Convention of 1832 declared that "as the Holy Communion is of a 'spiritually sacrificial' character, the standing posture should be observed by him, wherever that of kneeling is not expressly prescribed." [18] He should therefore stand, not kneel, while saying his pre-

---

[18] *Journal of the General Convention,* 1832, p. 451.

paratory prayers. He should stand also while receiving his Communion. He should kneel, as bidden by the rubric, when saying the Confession, in union with our Lord's kneeling in Gethsemane, as our Lord, being our representative Penitent, then knelt. He would kneel at the prayer, "We do not presume," etc., in memory of our Lord's falling under the Cross on the way to Calvary. He covers the elements after the consecration with a fair linen cloth, symbolical of our Blessed Lord's Body when taken down from the Cross being wrapped in a clean linen cloth and so laid in the tomb.

CEREMONIAL.

In the American Prayer Book, the Ornaments Rubric of England, which referred to the second year of the reign of King Edward VI., was naturally omitted. As we have seen, the omission would not mean any legalized change of ceremonial. What was legal in England would still be allowable in America. This is our authority for the use of the surplice, and if of the surplice, of the other clerical vestments. Thus the deacons at their ordination are to be "decently habited," the term "habit" being here used in its Liturgical sense,

"Let all things be done decently and in order." The retention by the Bishops of cope and mitre was declared to be legal by an official report to the House of Bishops concerning the Episcopal costume. The committee said, "the first Bishop of the American Church, Bishop Seabury, was accustomed to wear the mitre in certain offices, and the first of our Bishops ever consecrated in America, Bishop Claggett of Maryland, continued to do so." In connection with Bishop Seabury's wearing the mitre, the following anecdote may be interesting: Bishop Coxe wrote, learning that the mitre of Bishop Seabury, used in his Episcopal ministrations, was still in existence: "I had the curiosity to obtain it through the Rev. Dr. Seabury of New York, and placed it in the library of Trinity College. An aged priest, the Rev. Isaac Jones, came into the library, and on his betraying some emotion at the sight, I said to him, 'You have probably seen that mitre on Seabury's head.' He answered, 'Yes; in 1785, at the first ordination in this country, I saw him wearing a scarlet hood and that mitre.'" In the opinion of the committee above referred to, this historical fact justifies any Bishop in resuming it. This report was signed by the Rt. Rev. William C. Doane, Bishop of Albany; Rt. Rev. Arthur Cleveland Coxe, Bishop of Western New York; Rt. Rev. Henry C. Potter, Bishop of New York.[19]

Neither the use of the Eucharistic vestments nor the cope and mitre should be made a matter of party strife. Both High and Low Churchmen believe in the Apostolic character of our Church, and the vestments and other ornaments only bear witness to the continuity of our Church from Apostolic times. They are not introduced in the way of imitation of Rome, but as a protest against her exclusive claims. Whether their introduction is desirable was answered lately by a body of clergy in England in this wise: "The question whether the vestments should or should not be restored depends on whether it is desirable to exhibit or conceal the continuity which they express." In America, surrounded as we are by Romans and sectarians, is it not wise that we should declare, not by word only, but to the eyes of our people, that our Church is the same as that founded by the Apostles, and has come down to us through the ages?

---

[19] *Journal of Gen. Convention,* 1886, p. 795.

The Church's Title.

We come now to the *title of our Church*.

In 1785 the Church in America took for its legal title that of "Protestant Episcopal," but did not mean by that to deny that she was Catholic. The term Protestant has two significations. It may be used by those who, as members of a society, prefer not to leave but to remain in it under protest. In this way, our Church is a pro-testant Church. It protests against the additions made to the faith by Rome, and the subtractions made from it by sectarians. But it is not Protestant in the modern sense and use of the word, which involves a rejection of all Church authority and the sacramental system, and which has resulted in hundreds of sects. The Church in her government is "Episcopal." This distinguishes her from the Congregational, Presbyterian, and Papal systems. She believes that the government of the Church is vested in the Bishops and those under them. No one Bishop is independent of the others. His authority lies in his being a true exponent of the whole body of the Episcopate. We believe thus in the solidarity of the Episcopate. The authority that lies behind the individual Bishop is the corporate knowledge and consciousness of the whole undivided Church. The term "American Catholic" would now be more explicit in our attitude towards sectarians, and would discriminate us from the Roman Church. Our heritage in faith and worship, as expressed in our Book of Common Prayer, is a very grand and noble one. In these days, when Protestantism is disintegrating, and divisions are discernible in the Roman Communion, our Church, Apostolic and Orthodox, is being found a city of refuge. She has never placed herself, and does not now, in opposition to discovered facts of modern science. She does not repress reverent and scientific investigation of the construction of God's Word. She allows a certain amount of comprehensiveness by permitted diversities of ceremonial. We believe there is a growing spirit of union springing up within her. Men are outgrowing the little narrow prejudices which divided them into parties over trifling matters of ritual or speculative questions of doctrine.

We may, in conclusion, venture the criticism

that the Church has been heretofore too much on the defensive. Now no cause that is chiefly defensive will ever succeed. It must be constructive and aggressive in order to do so. There should therefore be an earnest and united effort made to gain a more appropriate title for our Church.

It belongs, moreover, to all her members to be true to the great trust they have received from their spiritual forefathers, and not allow it to be impaired, for the sake of popularity with the world, by compromise. As we have all received a great treasure which has come down to us through the sacrifices made by doctors, confessors, and martyrs, it becomes us to hand it on unimpaired to others. As our spiritual forebears made tremendous sacrifices of life and fortune that we might receive this inheritance of the Faith, we must in like manner make sacrifices for the benefit of coming generations. What our members especially need is to be more fully instructed in the history, doctrine, and worship of the Church, to be more and more united together in the bonds of Christian fellowship, to work for the Church as the greatest cause life can present to us, to use all its means of grace, and to love it with all their hearts.

The writer of this work prays that it may in its way aid to this blessed consummation. Our Church holds a magnificent position, and has great opportunities before her. We venture concerning her, to paraphrase the hymn of America's great poet:

> Sail on! O Church so true and tried,
> Afflicted sore, yet purified.
> The world and Satan's hosts unite
> Against thy witness to Christ's life.
> Humanity with all its fears,
> Its doubts, yet hopes for future years,
> Looks largely to thy heavenly aid.
> We know the Master laid the keel,
> Reformers wrought thy ribs of steel.
> What scaffolds bled, what martyrs died,
> In what a forge and pains beside
> Were shaped the anchors of thy hope!
> Thy compass is God's Holy Word,
> Thy freight the ancient faith untold:
> Fear not each sudden sound and shock,
> 'Tis of the wave and not the rock;
> In spite of Rome and tempest's roar,
> In spite of false lights on the shore,
> Sail on, nor fear to breast the sea!
> Our hearts, our hopes are all with thee.
> Our hearts, our hopes, our prayers, our tears,
> Our faith triumphant o'er our fears,
> Are all with thee, are all with thee!

BOOKS MADE USE OF IN CHAPTER IX.

Annals of the Low Church Party. Proby.
Tracts of the Times.
Life of Pusey. Liddon.
Pusey and the Church Revival. Grafton.
Life of Keble.
Life of Isaac Williams.
Letters of J. Mason Neale. E. A. Towle.
Lives of Charles Lowder, Mackonochie, and Others.
History of the English Church Union. Roberts.
Life of the Rev. Mother Superior of Clewer.
Three Hundred Years of American Church History. Hodges.
History of the Church in Maryland. Dr. Hawks.
History of the Church in Virginia.
History of the American Church. Coleman.
History of the American Church. McConnell.
Lives of Bishops White, Hobart, Seabury, Chase, Kemper.
Journals of the General Convention.